Bury St Edmunds
Market Cross

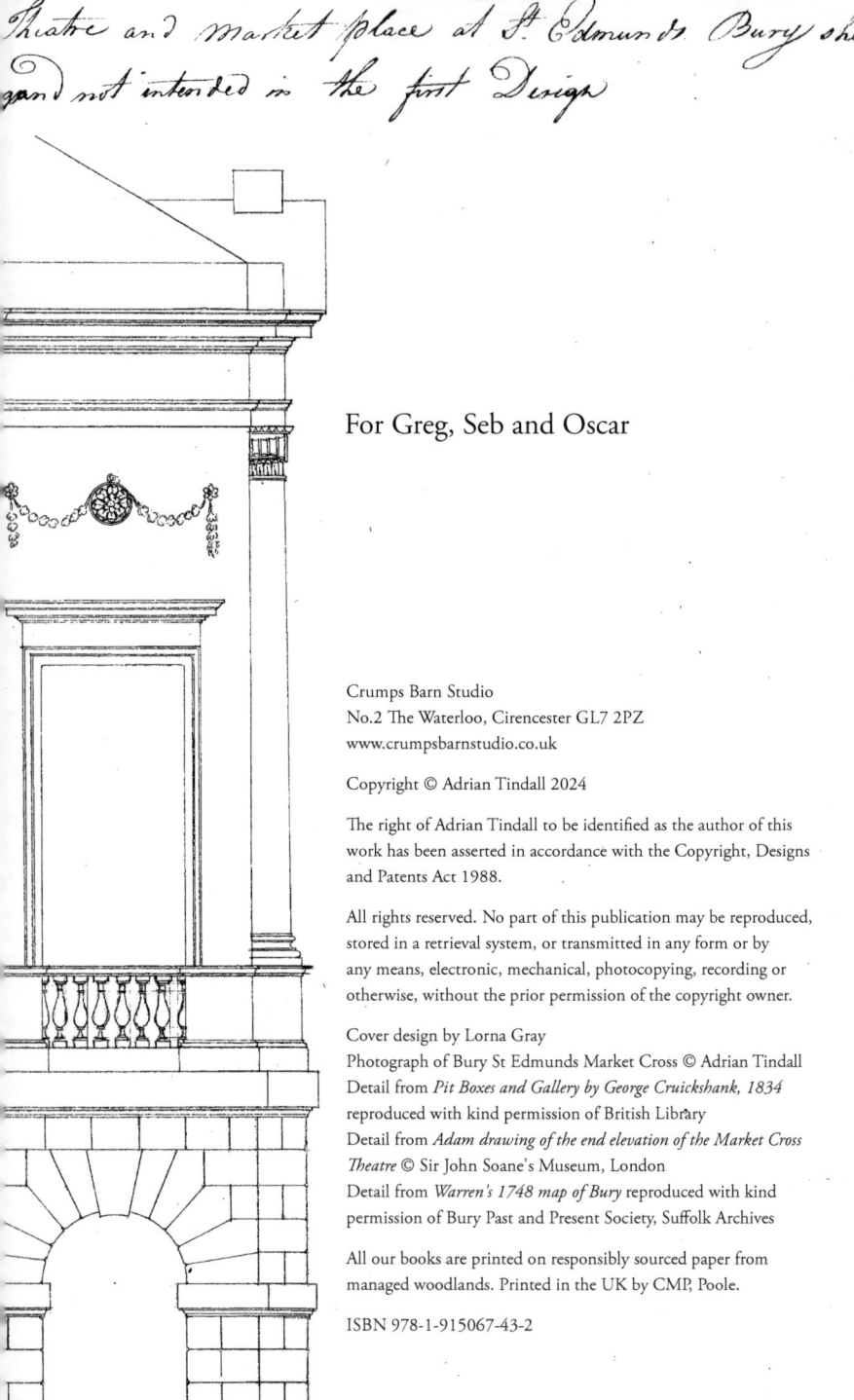

For Greg, Seb and Oscar

Crumps Barn Studio
No.2 The Waterloo, Cirencester GL7 2PZ
www.crumpsbarnstudio.co.uk

Copyright © Adrian Tindall 2024

The right of Adrian Tindall to be identified as the author of this work has been asserted in accordance with the Copyright, Designs and Patents Act 1988.

All rights reserved. No part of this publication may be reproduced, stored in a retrieval system, or transmitted in any form or by any means, electronic, mechanical, photocopying, recording or otherwise, without the prior permission of the copyright owner.

Cover design by Lorna Gray
Photograph of Bury St Edmunds Market Cross © Adrian Tindall
Detail from *Pit Boxes and Gallery by George Cruickshank, 1834* reproduced with kind permission of British Library
Detail from *Adam drawing of the end elevation of the Market Cross Theatre* © Sir John Soane's Museum, London
Detail from *Warren's 1748 map of Bury* reproduced with kind permission of Bury Past and Present Society, Suffolk Archives

All our books are printed on responsibly sourced paper from managed woodlands. Printed in the UK by CMP, Poole.

ISBN 978-1-915067-43-2

projections of the new Shops proposed to be joined to the sides of

'A Neat and Beautiful THEATRE':

The story of
Bury St Edmunds
Market Cross

ADRIAN TINDALL

Crumps Barn Studio

The History, the ACTORS, and the ARCHITECT ROBERT ADAM

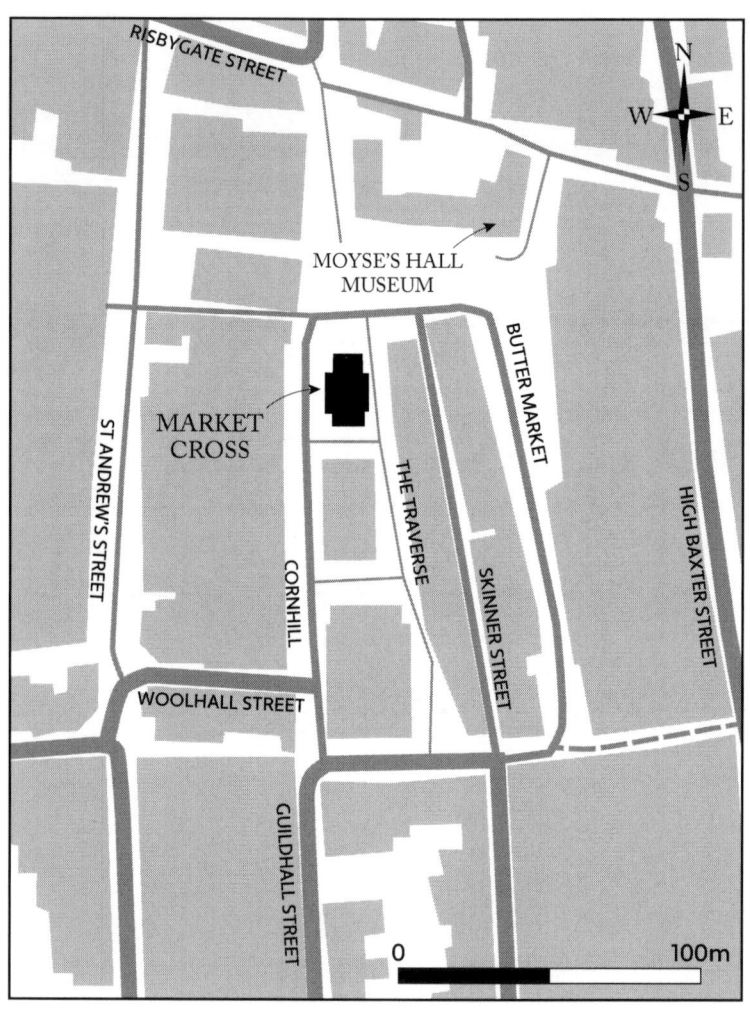

Map of Bury St Edmunds, showing location of the Market Cross (scale approx. 1:2500)

INTRODUCTION

ANY VISITOR TO Bury St Edmunds marketplace cannot fail to notice a handsome neoclassical building of white brick and limestone, standing on Cornhill opposite Moyse's Hall Museum. This is the Grade I Listed Bury St Edmunds Market Cross.

The Market Cross probably began life as a medieval preaching cross and corn exchange, became Bury's first playhouse, was redesigned as a Georgian theatre by one of Britain's foremost architects, and was later transformed into a Victorian concert room and town hall and, briefly, an art gallery.

The present building was designed in 1774 by the celebrated architect Robert Adam. 2024 therefore marks the 250th anniversary of Bury Corporation commissioning him to design what has been described by Sir Nikolaus Pevsner as *"the finest post-medieval building in Bury"*.

This book tells the story of the many incarnations of the Market Cross, and of some of the personalities who used, enjoyed or helped to shape it.

The original medieval market cross was probably similar to the stone market cross at Lavenham (Gail Preller)

THE MEDIEVAL MARKET CROSS

ONE OF THE questions most often asked about the Market Cross, is how it got its rather curious name. Although cruciform in plan, it does not seem to resemble a cross in the conventional sense of the word. The answer is rooted in its medieval origins.

Market crosses were common features of most medieval market towns. The earliest examples were probably simple wooden crosses, placed at or near the centre of the market. They originally served a multiple purpose: for preaching the gospel to the townsfolk, issuing public proclamations, witnessing acts of penance, forming a meeting point for traders, and providing a visible symbol of the Christian principles of fair trading.

Few if any wooden market crosses survive today. Just as the timber castles of the Norman Conquest were succeeded by medieval stone castles, so the earliest timber crosses were replaced in the later medieval period by stone crosses. These remained the focal point of the marketplace, with the same functions of preaching, proclamation and trade, but were more prominent and elaborate than their wooden predecessors, often being raised on two or three tiers of stone steps.

Bury's original Anglo-Saxon 'Horse Market', or 'Old Market' had long been held in the area around St Mary's

Square. However, following the establishment of the Benedictine Abbey of St Edmund under Cnut in 1020, the powerful Abbot Baldwin and a successor Anselm laid out a new Great Market as part of the Norman planned town of Bury St Edmunds, between the years 1065 and 1148.

The Great Market was originally a vast open space, extending from Moyse's Hall in the north to the present Abbeygate Street in the south, and from Buttermarket in the east to Cornhill in the west, covering a rectangular area of some 1.6ha (4 acres). Like the abbey precinct itself, the enormous size of the marketplace was an indication of the power and influence of the abbot. It also reflected the agricultural prosperity of its hinterland, based on corn, wool and cloth.

As was common at the time, the market was subdivided into different zones, according to the produce being traded. These included the beast, butter, wool, spice and fish markets. The corn market lay at the northern end of the marketplace, in the area which later became known as Cornhill.

It is difficult today to imagine the marketplace as one large open space. This is because later 'island' development, first in the form of temporary stalls and later as permanent buildings, has gradually infilled the area. It was further subdivided into smaller plots by The Traverse and the narrow medieval backstreet of Skinner Lane, now Skinner Street.

We have no record of what Bury's medieval Market Cross might have looked like. It was probably a stepped cross, like the surviving example at nearby Lavenham, built in 1502 and also probably replacing a timber cross. The exact location of Bury's cross is unknown, although the present Market Cross stands in a dominant position at the highest point of the Great Market, and so this is likely to have been the site of the original cross.

*Bury St Edmunds Market Cross
(Brian Mawdsley/Historic England)*

THE TUDOR MARKET CROSS

FOLLOWING THE ENGLISH Reformation in the 16th century, market crosses became less religious and more secular and commercial in character. In many cases the cross itself was removed and replaced with an open-sided shelter for traders of corn and other goods.

This was the case in Bury, where in 1583 the stones of the old Bury Market Cross were sold for £2, and the Guildhall Feoffees (charitable forerunners of the corporation) raised enough money to build:

> a very fayer large house for cornsellers … wherein they may stand to their great ease verye comodiouslye in the heate of Somer and also in the tyme of reynye and cold wet winter.
>
> *(Statham 1988, 89)*

The Bury Market Cross was probably an open wooden shelter protected by a lead roof, similar to the 15th century hexagonal example surviving at Mildenhall. It does not appear to have been very well built, as only twenty years later it was in disrepair, requiring the Feoffees to spend a further £2 on repairs and *"scruses and shores to uphowld the same"*.

*The 15th century hexagonal market cross at Mildenhall
(Suffolk News)*

THE
𝔚oefull and 𝔏amentable
wast and spoile done by a suddaine
Fire in S. Edmonds-bury in
Suffolke, on Munday, the tenth
of Aprill. 1 6 0 8.

LONDON
Printed for *Henrie Gosson,* and are to be solde in Pater-
noster rowe, at the Signe of the Sunne.
1 6 0 8.

THE GREAT FIRE OF BURY

FIRE WAS A constant threat in the closely-packed streets of timber and thatched houses in the towns of medieval England. It has been estimated that in the years between 1500 and 1800, there were over 500 major fires in England's towns and cities *(Garrioch, 204)*.

In East Anglia, such fires affected not only large cities such as Norwich (1507), but also smaller towns like Beccles (1586), Southwold (1659), Newmarket (1683) and Bungay (1688). The threat of fire was also increased where industrial processes, such as baking, malting or brewing, were carried out in urban areas.

This was the case in Bury, when fire broke out in James Randall's malthouse on Eastgate Street between 8 and 9am on Monday 10th April 1608. Fanned by a westerly wind, the fire spread up Northgate Street and Looms Lane to the marketplace. It burned for three days, and attempts to douse it emptied all the nearby ponds and wells. It was eventually stopped by demolishing houses in its path and by pulling off the thatch from roofs with long-handled metal hooks or 'cromes' to create a firebreak.

The fire was reported in a puritanical pamphlet published in London under the title:

THE
Woefull and Lamentable
wast and spoile done by a suddaine
Fire in S. Edmonds-bury in
Suffolke, on Munday, the tenth
of Aprill. 1608.

The pamphlet includes a stylised engraving of an urban fire, and concludes that it was the result of "*a remiss and sleepy negligence of a servant*" and divine retribution for the "*secret sins and offences*" of the townspeople – the invariable puritanical response to such tragedies.

The Market Cross itself was destroyed, the pamphlet recording that:

> The lead of the Market crosse and the crosse itself, was utterly ruinate and consumed to the ground by the violent blow of this hot encounter.

The fire is estimated to have destroyed around 160 dwellings and 400 outhouses, cellars and warehouses, consuming property, goods and livestock worth between £60,000 and £100,000. It effectively removed the central and eastern quarters of the medieval town although, miraculously, no human lives were lost.

Two years earlier, James I had granted Bury its first charter, creating a corporation of an alderman and 36 burgesses. Following the fire, the new corporation acted quickly, passing a byelaw to prohibit thatch being used on any new buildings within the town and requiring high-risk businesses such as maltsters to maintain approved leather 'tankards' or fire buckets.

In July 1608 the king granted the town a second charter ('The Market Charter'), giving the corporation the rights and tolls of Bury's market and fairs. It also granted them Bury Gaol, the toll house, the market cross *"lately ruined by fire"* and market bell, together with 500 tons of timber from Hitcham Wood to help rebuild the town.

With the aid of this grant, and with the customary donations from local church collections, rebuilding of the town began. One of the first houses to be rebuilt on Cornhill in 1609 was reputedly marked by a plaque bearing in Latin the couplet *"Burgus ut antiquus violento corruit igne, Hic stet dum flammis terra polusque flagranto" (McCutcheon, 35)*. This roughly translates as *"Tho furious fire the old Town did consume, Stand this till all the world shall flaming flume"*. A 19th century copy of this plaque still survives on the front of a shop on Cornhill.

One condition of the Market Charter was that the corporation must repair the town gaol and bridges and, at their own expense, *"build a Market Cross for the placing and exposing of grain and other commodities"*.

*The Jacobean Market Cross, detail from Downing's
1741 map of Bury (Moyse's Hall Museum)*

THE JACOBEAN MARKET CROSS

FOLLOWING THE FIRE, a temporary wooden cross was erected in the area of the market formerly known as 'Rotten Row' *(Statham 1988, 89)*. However by 1620 this had been replaced by an elaborate new timber-framed Market Cross on the present site. A view of this new Market Cross from the south-west is shown on Alexander Downing's 1741 map of Bury, where it is proudly featured in a framed inset or 'cartouche'.

It is shown as a substantial, detached, two-storeyed timber building. It had an open arcaded corn exchange (or *'cornstead'*) on the ground floor and a high, possibly galleried, clothiers hall above. The upper storey was served by a broad, partly-external staircase, with a veranda and balcony above, on what was the building's south and principal front. It was gabled, with a plaintiled roof, with decorative finials on each gable and an elaborate central cupola topped by a weathervane.

Cupolas were often added to larger buildings, usually to improve lighting and ventilation to the upper stories or to provide a viewpoint, or 'belvedere'. However, in Bury's case, the hexagonal louvred cupola may have served another purpose – as a belfry to house the market bell referred to in the 1608 Market Charter. Bells were an important feature of early markets, signalling the opening and closing of the day's trading, a tradition later reflected in the bells of the London and New York stock exchanges.

On the principal gable was a clock (possibly a later addition), and on the balcony rail the Royal coat of arms of James I, presumably in recognition of his incorporation of the town and support for its rebuilding after the fire. The coat of arms shows the unicorn on the left in the Scottish tradition, rather than on the right in the English. The balcony was presumably used for public proclamations, and the Market Cross was clearly an important municipal building, and a powerful expression of both civic pride and loyalty to the crown.

A view of the Market Cross from the south is also shown on Thomas Warren the Elder's 1748 map of Bury. This shows broadly the same features as on Downing's map, except that the first-floor balcony is now shown with a central door and transom window, flanked on either side by two porthole windows. A door would have been necessary to provide access to the balcony, and its omission from Downing's illustration seems to have been an oversight.

Few such timber market crosses survive today, having mostly been replaced (or in Bury encased) by later stone buildings. There seems to have been a fashion for building new market halls during the reign of James I, particularly in the years 1609—1622. Surviving examples include Dunster, Somerset (1609), Llanidloes, Powys (1612), Market Harborough, Leicestershire (1614), Ledbury, Herefordshire (1617), and Wymondham, Norfolk (1617) – all broadly contemporary with Bury's Market Cross. Whether this reflects a growth in municipal pride, a development in market economics or merely a natural consequence of urban fire risk is unclear.

As was the case in Bury, the upper floor of market halls was often used, at least initially, for trading in textiles. This is seen elsewhere, for example in the wool and flannel market at Llanidloes and the yarn market at Dunster.

Little is known of the early history of the new Market Cross, beyond occasional references to it in the corporation minutes. In 1622, the harvest failed, and the corporation paid 11s 5d for "*bord and workemanshipp for a bing [bin] at the Market Crosse to putt in meale to serve the poore*". During this time, parts of the open ground floor and upper rooms were leased out as shops; in July 1625, for example, £1 3s 8d for wood nails, etc was "*leyde out for the coblers shop under the crosse*". In 1670, the corporation minutes mention the provision of a new bushel (8 gallon measure) and chain, presumably for measuring grain, and the 1681 minutes mention the repair of the cross gallery.

In 1698, the renowned English traveller and writer Celia Fiennes visited Bury St Edmunds and noted that "*The Market Cross has a dyal and lanthorn [cupola] on the top*". She also admired nearby Cupola House, "*another house pretty close to it, high built with such a tower and lanthorn also*" (Morris, 139). A contemporary oil painting of the town in Moyse's Hall Museum shows the Market Cross dominating Cornhill, framed to the south-west by a row of taverns, and to the south-east by Cupola House and the beast market.

During this period, the Market Cross seemed perfectly suited to carry out all its civic and commercial functions. So what prompted the corporation to decide in October 1733 that the town needed a permanent theatre, and to consider converting the Market Cross for this purpose?

The Jacobean Market Cross, detail from Warren's 1748 map of Bury (Bury Past and Present Society, Suffolk Archives K505 3592)

EARLY THEATRE IN BURY ST EDMUNDS

MEDIEVAL AND TUDOR THEATRE

BURY HAS HAD a long association with theatre, beginning with the 'Mystery Plays' of the medieval period. Mystery Plays were biblical stories, presented as a series of plays in dramatic and sometimes comic form, often in cycles lasting several days. They were performed periodically by members of the guilds (or 'mysteries'), the associations of craftsmen and merchants in each town.

As early as 1389, when the dominance of the abbey was increasingly being challenged by the growing power of Bury's merchant guilds, the guild of Corpus Christi performed a short play in St James' Church on Corpus Christi Day, the Thursday after Trinity Sunday. The cost of producing such a play probably fell upon the guild members.

Complete versions of Mystery Plays have survived from York, Chester, Wakefield and Coventry. However the exact location of a further cycle, known as the 'N-Town Plays', remains unknown. This cycle may have been performed by travelling players, moving from town to town. However, Gibson *(1981)* has suggested that the N-Town Plays, performed in 1477 at the Corpus Christi festival by the linen and woollen weavers guild, may have been a Bury St Edmunds Mystery Cycle. This theory is based partly on their East Anglian dialect and partly on the presence in the abbey at that time of the monk and celebrated poet and dramatist John Lydgate.

A Coventry Mystery Play

The theory is supported by the ordinances (or rules) of the guild of woollen and linen weavers of Bury, drawn up in 1477. These stipulated that any breach of the rules should be punished by a fine, half of which would be devoted to:

> the sustenation and maintenance of the pageant of the Association of our Lord God and of the gifts of the Holy Ghost, and it has been accustomed of old time out of mind yearly to be performed for the worship of God, among other pageants in the procession of the feast of Corpus Christi.
>
> *(Statham 1970, 1)*

Mystery Plays were usually performed outdoors on wheeled floats or 'pageants', which would proceed in convoy through the town, with the players stopping to perform at fixed points, often to a boisterous audience. The suggestion that Mystery Plays were performed in Bury is supported by a Bury Guildhall Inventory of 1558, which records that pageant wagons were stored there, though were perhaps no longer in use *(Statham 1970, 1)*.

After the English Reformation of the 16th century, Mystery Plays began to fall out of favour, to be replaced by more secular forms of theatre. Troupes of travelling players would tour the fairs, inns and markets of Tudor England, performing both new and traditional comedies and tragedies.

In Bury, travelling players performed Shakespearean works, either in theatre 'booths' on Angel Hill or on makeshift stages in the galleried yards of local inns. One example may have been the galleried yard of the now-lost *Half Moon* coaching inn at 28 Buttermarket, and it has been suggested *(Statham 1988, 104)* that *The One Bull* on Angel Hill may have been another.

This practice was clearly widespread, because in 1607 the newly-established corporation passed a by-law prohibiting such performances without a licence:

> Item to prevent the resort of idle persons to plays and sights of toys it is ordered that no Innholder, Alehousekeeper, Victualler or any other person inhabiting within this Borough shall permit or suffer any stage play, comedy, interlude, or other play to be played in their or any of their houses or any horses, baboons, apes, bears, puppets or other sights or shows to be made in their or any of their houses upon pain of forfeit for the first offence £3 6s 8d, and for the second offence £6 13s 4d, and for the third offence £10. 0s 0s, without the licence of the Alderman, Recorder and Assistants or two of them thereunto first had and obtained in writing.
>
> *(Statham 1970, 1)*

These heavy fines perhaps reflect the corporation's rather puritanical view of theatrical performance, a view which was widely held before the Restoration of Charles II in 1660.

Other outdoor spaces were also used for theatrical performance. In 1639, a play was performed by the boys of the

King Edward VI Grammar School 'at the abbey' *(Statham 1988, 104)*, though the exact location of this performance is unknown.

Half-Moon Yard, Bury c. 1870
(Bury Past and Present Society K505 537)

EARLY GEORGIAN THEATRE

DURING THE 1720s, the *Suffolk Mercury* records several visits during the Bury Fair by Henry Tollet's Company of Comedians, performing at 'the Shire House', probably the Grand Jury House. Their productions included *The*

Fond Husband; or The Plotting Sisters: a Comedy by Thomas D'Urfey (written in 1677), *Vertue Betrayed; or Anna Bullen: a Tragedy* by John Banks (1682) and *Oroonoko: or the Royal Slave: A True History* by Aphra Behn (1688).

It has been suggested *(Statham 1970, 2)* that 'the Shire House' may have been *"the little country opera-house in St Edmund's Bury"* referred to in Daniel Defoe's 1722 novel *Moll Flanders*, where Moll recounts how she *"made a shift to carry off a gold watch from a lady's side, who was not only intolerably merry, but, as I thought, a little fuddled, which made my work much easier."*

We know that Defoe himself visited Bury early in 1722 as part of his *Tour Through the Whole Island of Great Britain* (1724).

In 1725, the scholars of the Grammar School performed Terence's comedy *The Brothers* in the original Latin, and Brome's 1629 comedy, *The Northern Lass; or The Nest of Fools* *"to the admiration of the Quality and Gentry"*, also at the Shire House.

There were also rival attractions to conventional theatre. In May 1725, *"the Quality and Gentry"* were entertained during the Bury Races by Powell's Puppet Theatre of Bath *(Grice, 144)*. Indeed, companies of puppets and variety shows ('medleys') were highly popular, and often included acrobats, dancers, conjurors and even waxworks.

On 21 September 1726, a 'Grand Theatrical Booth' was set up in in the 'Abbey Yard' (probably the Abbey Gardens), and Henry Tollet's Company of Comedians announced that:

they would perform there during the Bury Fair time all the most celebrated Tragedies and Comedies. Lamps would be provided for the convenience of coaches at the Abbey Gate and elsewhere ... and a good band of musick.

In 1727, A Company of Comedians (possibly again Henry Tollet's) performed Colley Cibber's 1696 Restoration Comedy *Love's Last Shift* in the North Hall of the Guildhall, for the benefit of Mr and Mrs Paul. The following year they returned to perform William Congreve's 1693 Restoration Comedy *The Old Bachelor*.

In 1728, 'The Norwich Company of Comedians, Servants to his Grace the Duke of Grafton' (which had been formed two years earlier) performed John Gay's new work *The Beggar's Opera* during the Bury Fair, possibly again in the North Hall of the Guildhall. This three-act satirical ballad opera was hugely successful, becoming perhaps the most popular play of the 18th century. It helped to popularise a satirical version of *Lillibullero*, sung by the highwayman character, Macheath.

In 1733 the *Suffolk Mercury* carried advertisements for performances by the Norwich Company of Comedians at 'the Play-house' in Risbygate Street *(Statham 1988, 104)*, perhaps another inn-yard venue.

Most of these early performances by travelling players were staged to coincide with the celebrated Bury Fair, held every year around the Feast of St Matthew (21 September) and often lasting several weeks. Originally granted to Abbot Anselm by Henry I in the 1140s as a week-long fair for the exchange of wool and cloth, the Bury Fair had by the Georgian period become one of the most fashionable events of the social calendar. Indeed, so famous had it become that playwright Thomas Shadwell, a former pupil of the Grammar School, wrote a play very loosely based around it called *Bury Fair*, first performed by Thomas Betterton's Company at London's Drury Lane Theatre in 1689.

Hone's 1773 Yearbook describes the Bury Fair as:

> more a place of amusement than a temporary Mart, as most of the Merchandises now brought thither are chiefly Articles of Luxury and Curiosity. It is held on a spacious plain, betwixt the magnificent Gate of the Abbey and the town; it begins the twenty-first of September, and lasts fourteen days. It is the rendezvous of the beau monde every afternoon, who conclude their evenings by the plays or assemblies. This fair consists chiefly of several rows of haberdashers, milliners, mercers, jewellers, silversmiths and toy shops, which make a fine show.

The fair was the centrepiece and main stimulus of the town's Georgian renaissance. Since the dissolution of the abbey in 1539, Bury had reverted to the role of a peaceful and prosperous market town. However, in the Georgian period the town reinvented itself as a place of resort for 'The Better Sort': the fashionable landowning gentry, who were enjoying the new prosperity and high disposable income of that expansive age. Every autumn they descended on Bury, from

East Anglia and beyond, to take the air and to enjoy the pleasures of the fair, the assemblies, the races, the plays and, of course, the matchmaking.

Although not a spa town, Daniel Defoe in his *Tour Through the Whole Island of Great Britain (1724, 73)* describes Bury's other attractions:

> It is a town famed for its pleasant situation and wholesome air, the Montpelier of Suffolk, and perhaps of England ... it being the town of all this part of England, in proportion to its bigness, most thronged with gentry, people of the best fashion, and the most polite conversation.

Its attractions as a fashionable resort were enhanced by its 'picturesque' antiquity, its affluence and its judicial and municipal prestige. Its location was also crucial, standing at the centre of a road network with regular coach services to London, Yarmouth, Norwich, Cambridge and Colchester, and in close proximity to the fashionable racing town of Newmarket *(Fiske 1990, 192).*

By the 1730s, theatre had become an essential feature of the Bury social season. It was becoming clear that a permanent theatre was now needed, to meet the demands of these more genteel theatregoers and to replace the various *ad hoc* venues that had previously served the town.

THE FIRST MARKET CROSS PLAYHOUSE

IN OCTOBER 1733 the corporation agreed that it needed to provide a permanent theatre in the town and ordered that a committee *"Doe inspect and look over the Market Crosse within this Burgh in order for making the same into a Playhouse"*.

The committee reported favourably, and on 14 January 1734, the corporation minutes record that:

> they have viewed the common cross within the Burgh and consulted with able and experienced workmen concerning the same, and are of opinion it may very conveniently and with safety be made a Playhouse. And the expense thereof will be about one hundred and fifty pounds.

It was therefore agreed to convert the clothiers hall on the upper storey of the Market Cross into a new playhouse, in doing so creating one of the earliest municipal theatres in England. This conversion represented a radical change for the Market Cross, from its sacred medieval origins to the often bawdy irreverence of the Georgian stage. Bury was not unique in this respect: at the Market House in Ledbury,

Herefordshire, bands of strolling players enacted plays in the ground floor market arcade, and by the 1830s were performing in the great hall above.

The workmen engaged by the corporation to carry out the work were local men Thomas Hawes, James Hasted and William Steel whose quote, submitted two days previously, was £150 4s 4d. The fitting out of the new playhouse took over seven months, but in September 1734 the *Grubstreet Journal* reported that:

> our workmen are very near drawing to a conclusion the finishing of the Grand Theatre, which has been so long fitting up here, for His Grace the Duke of Grafton's company of comedians; and when the paintings and everything are completed it is believed it will equal (if not exceed) any in England, and none can be supposed to come near it for situation; the company are to come from the University of Cambridge, to open it the beginning of our next fair.

The new playhouse was initially leased on 10 August 1734 to George Steggould, for seven years at £42 per year. Under the terms of the lease, he could use the playhouse from 20 September to 10 October for the Bury Fair, from 26 December to 12 January for Christmas performances, and a fortnight for performances during the quarterly Bury Assizes. This set the annual pattern for both the playhouse and its successor, neither of which was in active use for more than a few weeks of the year.

On 21 September 1734, a notice in the *Suffolk Mercury* announced that His Grace the Duke of Grafton's (later the Norwich) Company of Comedians

> will certainly be here Tuesday next, in order to open the Corporation theatre on Wednesday Night next (25th September) and intend to begin with the same diverting comedy which gained so much Applause, the first Night at the University of Cambridge call'd The Married Philosopher [John Kelly's 1732 comedy] … And intend to perform a select Number of PLAYS during their stay here, which were never performed here before.
>
> *(Green, 6)*

Other plays that first season included Thomas Otway's 1680 domestic tragedy *The Orphan: or The Unhappy Marriage*, Henry Fielding's 1732 comedy *The Mock Doctor: or The Dumb Lady Cur'd* and Joseph Addison's 1712 *Cato: A Tragedy*.

The Norwich Company of Comedians were to become the resident company at the Market Cross playhouse for over 80 years, before moving to the newly-built Theatre Royal in 1819. However this did not prevent its use by others.

On 24 October 1734 the corporation offered free use of the playhouse to scholars of the Free Grammar School, on condition that they made good any damage to the seats and scenery. In November they presented Ben Johnson's 1605 comedy *Volpone* and Plautus' *Pseudolus,* in the original Latin but with a specially-written prologue:

> Can ages past one single proof produce
> Of any playhouse born without a muse?
> Will future ages without pain believe
> Bury so strange a precedent should give?
> Is Bury blest with no poetic minds?
>
> *(Green, 8)*

At this time there were parliamentary efforts to regulate public theatrical performances. In 1737 a Licensing Act was passed prohibiting performances except in 'Patent Theatres', ie those theatres holding either a Lord Chamberlain's licence or a Royal Patent. Anyone disobeying this law would be deemed '*a Rogue and a Vagabond*'. However, there were many breaches of the law, and its loopholes were widely exploited. For example, the law did not apply to musical performances, and so theatrical performances were often disguised as concerts, with a free 'theatrical interlude'. Subsequently the regulations were relaxed, when the Theatrical Representations Act of 1788 allowed local magistrates to license occasional performances for periods of up to sixty days.

In its early years there are sporadic references in the provincial press to the Norwich Company and the new Market Cross playhouse. In 1737 Mrs Bowman, a prominent member of the company, was reported to have been killed while travelling from Bury to Colchester. This was later denied by the company:

> The Report of the Death of Mrs Bowman, the Fam'd Actress in the Norwich Company of Comedians, is not true, for since the Waggon went over her Body going from Bury Fair to Colchester, she is so well rcover'd as to Play almost every Night.
>
> *(Rosenfeld, 293)*

On 3 September 1748, the corporation minutes record that £10pa was granted to the Bailiffs of the Fairs and Markets for "*sweeping and keeping clean the Market Cross within this Burgh.*"

In 1753, two tiers of boxes were introduced into the theatre, "*which was decorated in the most elegant manner*". The audience was also forbidden to sit on the stage, as previously "*the gallants of the town liked to sit on the stage on three-legged stools*" (Green, 8).

The Norwich Company productions in 1753 included James Ralph's 1731 tragedy *The Fall of the Earl of Essex* and Henry Fielding's 1730 tragedy *Tom Thumb*, with the title role played by Miss Hindes, aged 5. The following year, Mrs Saunders was acclaimed for her performances as Alice in Nicholas Rowe's *The Tragedy of Jane Shore* (1714) and as Ophelia in Joseph Peterson's production of *Hamlet*. In 1755, The company played at Bury both in May, with a revival of *The Beggar's Opera*, featuring Mr Moody as Macheath and Mrs Saunders as Polly Peachum, and at the Bury Fair with James Ralph's 1734 farce *The Cornish Squire*.

In October 1758, Joseph Peterson, a long-standing member of the Norwich Company, died while rehearsing his role as Duke Vincentio in *Measure for Measure*. He is reputed to have collapsed while reciting a speech from Act 3 Scene 1:

> "Reason this with life:
> If I do lose thee, I do lose a thing
> That none but fools would keep; a
>   breath thou art ..."

These words were reputedly carved on his tombstone in Bury's Great Churchyard *(Green, 8)*, though there may be some dramatic licence in this story. His 'much decayed' tombstone was last recorded by Rev Francis Haslewood in 1887 as bearing the inscription *"Here lie the remains of Mr Joseph Peterson, an esteemed and much regretted member of the Norwich Company"*. The grave is now lost, but the burial is recorded on 24 October 1758 in the Parish Register of St James, perhaps suggesting it originally lay in the northern part of the churchyard, close to St James' Church, now the Cathedral.

In 1762, the playhouse was leased to actor-manager William Crouse, who ran the Norwich Circuit for two years, before becoming its joint manager, in an uneasy relationship with Richard Griffith: Crouse was in charge of wardrobes and Griffith in charge of productions and players.

In 1773 the corporation's Committee of Repairs took over supervision of the Market Cross. The building was about to undergo a most dramatic transformation. On 6 June 1774, the corporation issued an order that *"the Playhouse over the Market Cross be repaired and a south end built of brick and stonework according to the Plan of Robert Adams [sic] Esquire."*

So who was Robert Adam, and how did he come to be entrusted with the redesign of Bury's Market Cross Playhouse?

Robert Adam's first commission in Bury St Edmunds was St Edmund's Hill, designed in 1773. South front, c. 1800 (RIBApix 153027)

ROBERT ADAM

ROBERT ADAM WAS a neoclassical architect and designer. He was also one of the most influential figures of the Scottish Enlightenment. He was born on 3rd July 1728, in Kirkaldy, Fife, the second son of Scotland's foremost architect, William Adam. Robert had a wealthy upbringing, and received a classical education at Edinburgh Royal High School and the University of Edinburgh.

When their father died in 1748, Robert and his elder brother John inherited the family architectural practice, including its lucrative military contract for the Board of Ordnance. Their work included the design and construction of the imposing new fortifications of Fort George, Inverness, following the 1745 Jacobite Rebellion.

In 1754, Adam embarked on a Grand Tour, the customary rite of passage for all aspiring artists and architects of the day. His tour took him via France to Italy, where in Rome he studied classical architecture at the French Academy under French draughtsman Charles-Louis Clérisseau and Italian artist and antiquary Giovanni Battista Piranesi. Unusually, Robert extended his tour to Dalmatia (Croatia), where he studied and recorded the ruins of Diocletian's Palace at Spolatro (Split).

In 1758 he settled in London where he set up an architectural practice with his brother James at 75 Lower Grosvenor Street, later moving to 13 Albemarle Street. Here he employed

10 to 12 draughtsmen, each paid £40 to £60 per year, some of whom, such as George Richardson and Joseph Bonomi, later became well-known architects in their own right. All finished drawings produced by the practice remained Adam designs, and were signed as such by the brothers.

It was here that Adam resolved to create *"the Antique, the Noble and the Stupendous"* (*Oxford Dictionary of National Biography [ODNB]*), in what was later to become known as the 'Adam Style'. This was typified by decorative neoclassical designs, with an emphasis on achieving harmony in its exteriors, interiors and furnishings. He rejected the more austere Palladian neoclassical style that tended towards strict symmetry on a monumental scale, in favour of a more picturesque quality, which was airy, light and lively. He used dramatic variety and irregularity of form to create the idea of 'movement' in his buildings and interiors.

His work was heavily influenced by the newly discovered archaeological remains of Pompeii and Herculaneum, and he collaborated closely with the leading furniture and cabinet makers of the day, including Thomas Chippendale and George Hepplewhite.

He was socially ambitious, and successfully courted a number of influential patrons, most notably John Stuart, 3rd Earl of Bute, a close friend of George III. Through his patronage, Adam served as MP for Kinross-shire from 1768—74, and proved happy to bend the truth to suit his ambitions, writing, *"A good lye well timed does well"* (*ODNB*).

In 1761 he was jointly appointed Architect of the King's Works, again through the Earl's influence. However his co-appointee William Chambers was a fierce rival, and excluded him from many royal and public commissions. Surviving examples of Adam's public work are the Admiralty Screen in Whitehall (1760) and Pulteney Bridge in Bath (1770).

Many of his commissions at the time were for large country houses, where he was often employed to redesign exteriors, interiors and furnishings in the new Adam Style. Examples included Kedleston Hall, Derbyshire (1759—65), Osterley Park, Middlesex (1761—1780), Syon House, Middlesex (1762—9), and Harewood House, Yorkshire (1759—71).

One such commission brought him to Bury St Edmunds, where in 1773 he designed St Edmund's Hill, an elegant country house on the eastern outskirts of the town. His client was John Symonds, agronomist, lawyer and Professor of Modern History at the University of Cambridge. The two men seem already to have been acquainted, since Symonds was one of the subscribers to Adam's 1764 volume on Diocletian's Palace at Spalatro. St Edmund's Hill was later renamed The Mount and is now the Grade II* Listed Moreton Hall School.

Adam also designed some important London town houses, such as Wynn House, St James Square (1772—4), Home House, Portman Square (1775—7), Derby House, Grosvenor Square (1773—4) and Fitzroy Square (1790—98).

Robert Adam's success provoked some hostility from his contemporaries, among whom he was often regarded as a flawed genius: arrogant, self-indulgent and, due to his diverse interests, something of a *dilettante*.

The Adam brothers were also administratively inept, particularly in financial affairs. In 1768 their design for Adelphi Terrace, a vast waterfront residential and warehouse development on The Strand, proved an overambitious and speculative disaster. They were eventually forced to lay off 3,000 men working on the project, and only a public lottery in 1774 raised sufficient funds to avert their bankruptcy. The architectural practice itself had moved to Royal Terrace in the Adelphi development in 1772.

The years following this bitter experience were lean ones for the practice, with fewer and often smaller commissions. It was partly to rebuild their reputation that the Adam brothers published two volumes of their architectural designs under the title *The Works in Architecture of Robert and James Adam*, in 1773—8 and 1779.

Robert Adam did, however, retain a keen interest in one specialised field of architectural design, the theatre. In 1775 he remodelled the Theatre Royal, Drury Lane for the actor-manager David Garrick. Sadly, none of his original work survives, though engravings of both the exterior and interior were published in Volume II of *The Works in Architecture* in 1779. The contemporary architect Sir John Soane, a notoriously fierce critic, described it as:

> what the architecture of the interior of a theatre should be; and what it could be, when directed by the mind of a genius. The decoration displayed a lively, rich fancy, and correct application of that lightness and variety so peculiarly adapted to theatrical architecture, which distinguished every part of the work.
>
> *(ODNB)*

Adam's Theatre Royal, Drury Lane Exterior

Adam's Theatre Royal, Drury Lane Interior

Adam later submitted an ambitious and creative design for the Haymarket Opera House in London, though this was never realized.

In 1774, Bury corporation invited designs for the new south front of Bury's Market Cross playhouse. Adam had only recently been commissioned to prepare a plan for a new Town Hall in Manningtree, but its financier had gone bankrupt and the project had unexpectedly fallen through. As a result, he was able to prepare and submit his design for the Bury Market Cross playhouse, approved by the corporation on Monday 6 June 1774.

*Adam's design for the new Market Cross theatre, 1774
(Moyse's Hall Museum)*

ROBERT ADAM'S NEW THEATRE

ROBERT ADAM'S ORIGINAL "*Design of a New Elevation of the Theatre at St Edmunds Bury in the county of Suffolk*" is still preserved in Bury's Moyse's Hall Museum. It is a beautifully-drawn pen and ink elevation of the proposed neoclassical south front, much as it appears today, though lacking any detail of the doors or fenestration. It must be remembered that all designs produced by the Adam office were signed by one or both of the Adam brothers, so the design may have been the work of one of their talented draughtsmen.

At this time, the corporation only intended to reface the principal, south elevation of the building, presumably for reasons of cost. However, in the months that followed, a more ambitious plan, to reface the entire building, began to emerge. This was assisted by some successful fund-raising; on 13 October 1774 George Hervey, 2nd Earl of Bristol, of Ickworth House, donated £500 towards "*repairing and beautifying of the New Theatre*".

Adam worked on the revised proposals, and by January 1775 had begun preparing pencil-drawn plans and elevations of the proposed building, some of which are preserved in Sir John Soane's Museum. These unfinished drawings show an enlarged neoclassical scheme, with a cruciform plan partially encasing the old timber-framed Market Cross, and with all four fronts of the building now refaced in Adam Style. The open arcaded ground floor was to be retained as a market cross, shelter and corn exchange, apart from two small shops at its northern end.

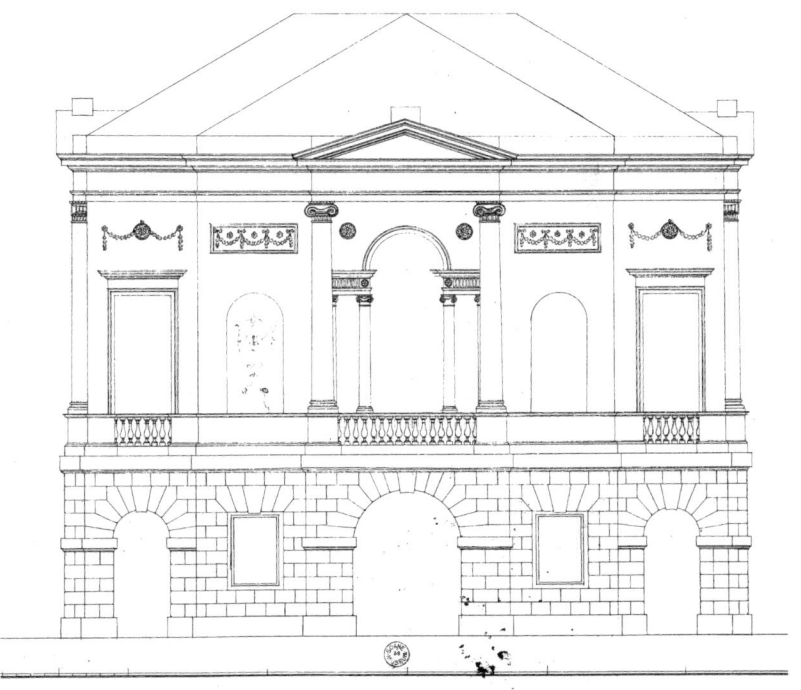

Adam drawing of the end elevation of the Market Cross Theatre (© Sir John Soane's Museum, London, Adam_38_038, Ardon Bar Hama)

The first elevation, drawn in the Adelphi office and dated 12 January 1775, is entitled:

> Design of a new elevation of the two ends of the Theatre and market place at St Edmunds Bury shewing the projections of the new slips proposed to be joined to the sides of the Building and not originally intended in the first Design

From this description it appears that the intention was to encase some of the principal timber beams of the existing building with brick cladding (or 'slips'), rather than to re-build it entirely.

The second elevation, again from the Adelphi office and bearing the same date, is headed: *Elevation of the two side Fronts of the Theatre and market place at St Edmunds Bury*

A third unfinished elevation of the north or south front is untitled and undated, but is presumably contemporary with the other two elevations.

The ground plan, unsigned and undated but presumably of similar date, is headed:

> Plan of the Market. Those parts that are shaded light shew the present building, and those that are shaded dark shew the additions proposed. The four piers that are marked A are proposed to be taken entirely away, and the eight piers marked B to be put up in order to keep the peircings opposite to the external Arches in the side Fronts, and must increase the strength of the building if executed with ingenuity. St Edmunds Bury

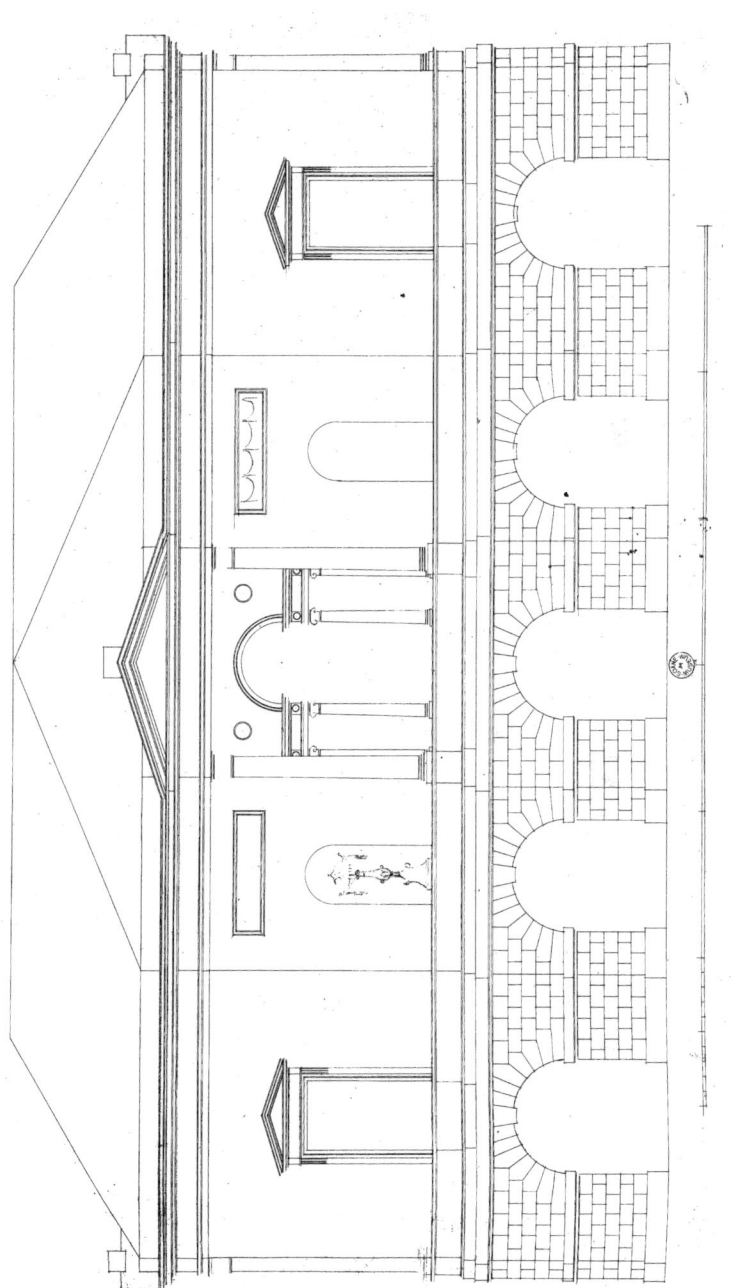

Adam drawing of the side elevation of the Market Cross Theatre (© Sir John Soane's Museum, London, Adam_38_039, Ardon Bar Hama)

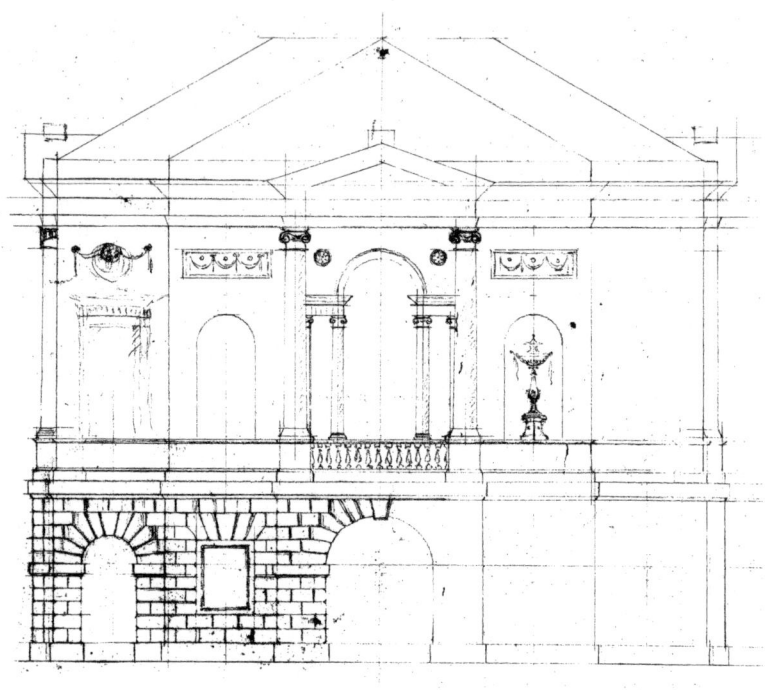

Adam unfinished drawing of the end elevation of the Market Cross (© Sir John Soane's Museum, London, Adam_38_040 verso, Ardon Bar Hama)

To the right (or south) is added a note *"Lobby with the stairs leading to the Theatre above"* and to the left are two small rooms labelled *"shops"*.

It again appears from this description that some of the principal timbers of the earlier Market Cross were to be retained and encased within the new building. Indeed, some of these were said to have been exposed during alterations to the building in the early 1970s *(Statham 1988, 94)*.

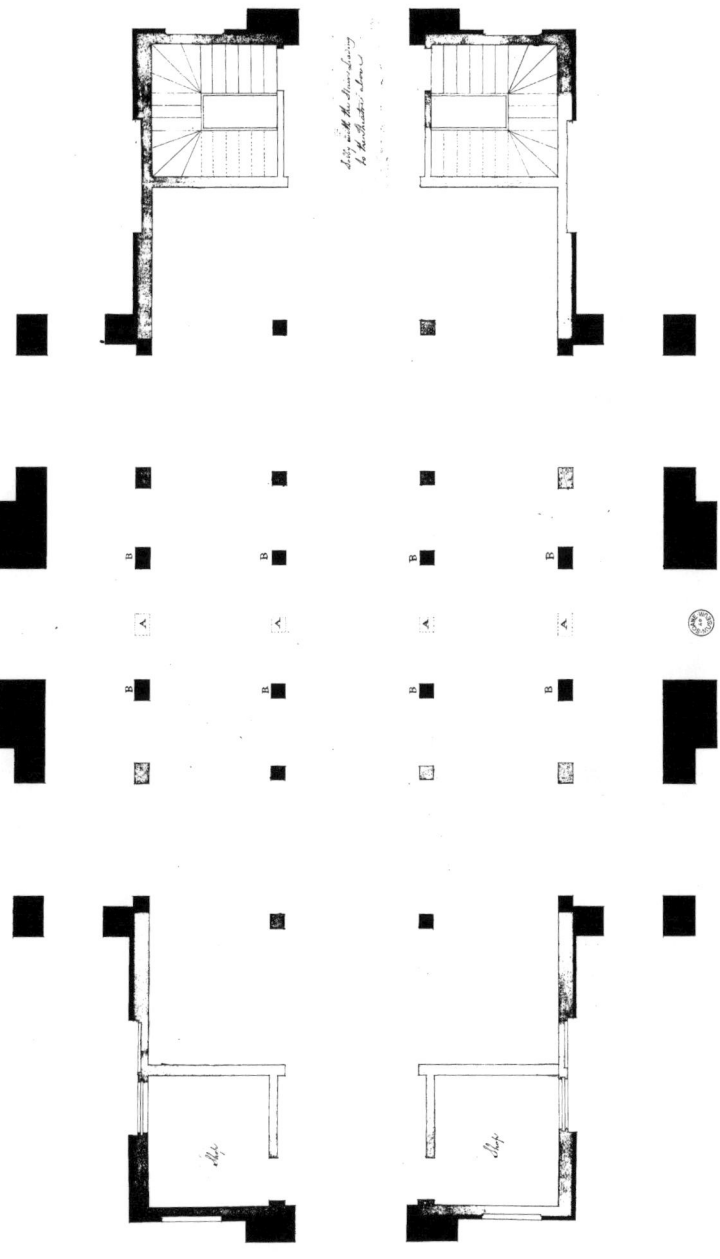

Adam plan of the Market Cross Theatre (© Sir John Soane's Museum, London, Adam_38_040, Ardon Bar Hama)

IN ANTICIPATION OF the new theatre's opening, the receiver of rents had already informed the Norwich Company by August 1774 that the annual rent for the *"Chamber and Buildings above the Market Cross with the stage, seats and appurtenances as the same are now fitted up"* would be £80 (it had previously been £45). However, this demand may have been premature, since the increased rent was not paid until October 1775, once the theatre was fully in use.

The new theatre was largely completed by 1776, when an illustration of its south front appears alongside other prominent Bury buildings on Thomas Warren the Younger's 2nd edition map of the town. Its inclusion among such well-known landmarks as St James' and St Mary's churches, the Abbey Gate, the Earl of Bristol's House (the Manor House), the Grand Jury House, the Grammar School and the Hospital (Clopton's Asylum) is perhaps an indication of both its novelty and significance. Neither the Bridewell (Moyse's Hall) nor the Assembly House (Athenaeum) is illustrated, though this need not be a significant omission: town maps in the Georgian period were increasingly funded by wealthy subscribers, who could influence decisions on which features of the town were to be highlighted.

During the period 1775—81, repeated sums were raised by the corporation's Repairing Committee for continuing work on the building. On 19 March 1779, the corporation also ordered that the Market Cross be *"guarded round and preserved by a proper iron palisade"*. The theatre was not finally completed until about 1780.

The scheme had originally been estimated at £2,500, which was to be paid through the Earl of Bristol's donation, and the sale of 400 individual bonds at £5 each. However, when building work was finally completed, the total cost had risen to £3,825, an extremely costly undertaking for the corporation. It was proposed that this sum would be funded by the Earl of Bristol's £500, plus £2,400 in loans and £925 in compulsory interest-free loans of £25 each from members of the corporation. Lots were drawn to decide the order in which the loans were to be repaid, but the process of repayment was slow; by 1796, only £800 of the loans had been repaid. Adam's bill for his design of the building had been 40 Guineas (£42), which was paid in 1777.

When the building was completed, it was described by a contemporary as *'a neat and beautiful Theatre' (Ashby, 75)*. Sir Nikolaus Pevsner, writing in the Suffolk volume of *The Buildings of England (Bettley and Pevsner, 144)* describes it as "*the finest post medieval building in Bury*".

It was designated a Grade I listed building of special architectural or historic interest in 1952. Grade I listed buildings are those of exceptional significance, and represent only 2.5% of all listed buildings in England. The full Official List Entry on the National Heritage List for England is given in the appendix.

THE DECISION TO choose an 'island' site was unusual for a theatre of the time, most of which were built into existing street frontages, and will have added significantly to its cost. The finished cruciform building is in typical Adam Style, with its rusticated pale yellow Ketton Limestone ground floor and its white Suffolk brick upper storey, topped by a stone cornice.

Venetian windows, Ionic *aediculae* (columns supporting a pediment and frieze), and the decorative swags, *paterae* and Etruscan vases, were again typical Adam Style neoclassical features. All the upper storey windows have ornamental stone balustrades, although many of the original windows have been replaced with later small-paned sash windows.

It has been pointed out *(Clifton-Taylor, 109)* that the glazing bars on the arched Venetian window-heads on the east and west fronts vary slightly from those on the north and south. Those on the east and west are classically radial, while those on the north and south unusually continue vertically through the centre of the arch. This may simply be due to the practical limitations of their width: the windows on the wider east and west fronts are nine lights wide, while those on the narrower north and south are reduced to only six lights wide.

Some of the decorative details on the exterior are of dressed limestone, but others such as the swags, *paterae* and Etruscan vases on the upper storey are made of cast iron and an artificial stone known as 'Coade stone'. Coade stone or *Lithodipyra* ('stone fired twice') was a type of moulded architectural stoneware invented by manufacturer Eleanor Coade in 1769, and produced by the Coade Artificial Stone Manufactory in Lambeth until 1833. For several decades it was highly fashionable and widely used for neoclassical ornaments and decorations on such prominent buildings as Brighton Royal Pavilion and St George's Chapel, Windsor.

The list entry identifies the decorative panels on either side of the doorways on the north and south fronts as masks and emblems representing the Muses. They were carved in

Ketton Limestone by respected local stonemason Thomas Singleton. He lived in the ostentatiously-decorated *St Denys* at 6 Honey Hill, and was responsible for work on several important buildings in Bury, including James Oakes's House and the Guildhall, both on Guildhall Street.

The two pairs of panels on the north and south faces of the building are nearly identical in design. They show a variety of musical instruments (flutes, lyres and horns), weapons (firearms, sabres and arrows) and keys. The masked images are usually interpreted as the Muses of Comedy and Tragedy, according to theatrical tradition, and indeed Adam's original drawings show the two panels without decorative detail but lightly marked in pencil with the words 'Comedy' and 'Tragedy'. It has been suggested *(Lansman, 43)* that the masks might also represent the horned god Pan and an unidentified king, possibly Midas, King of Phrygia. In Greek mythology, Midas is said to have judged a musical competition between the flute of Pan and the lyre of the god Apollo. He chose Pan, and Apollo punished him by giving him donkey's ears, so that he forever after wore long hair to conceal them.

A less obvious feature of the two Comedy panels is the indistinct outline of a page of musical notation, encircled by a horn to the right of the mask. This has been interpreted *(Lansman, 44)* as eight bars of 'God Save the King', beginning from the line '*Send him victorious* …'. If so, this would be the earliest known representation in stone of the National Anthem. The author and composer of the National Anthem is unknown, but it first appeared in print as *God Save Our Lord the King* in October 1745. Later that year, it was played by the orchestra and sung by the audience at both the

Theatre Royal, Drury Lane and the Theatre Royal, Covent Garden, supposedly in support of George II following his defeat by the Jacobite rebels at the Battle of Prestonpans in September 1745. This established the traditional association between theatrical performances and the singing of the National Anthem, a tradition which later extended to many other forms of live entertainment.

It is difficult now to imagine the original interior of the building, fully furnished with stage, pit, boxes and gallery. Although still exceptionally light and airy, the interior is now, due to its many changes of use, rather plain. It retains a few of its original features, such as the decorative plaster cornices with palmettes, the acanthus-leaf ceiling bosses and the moulded doors, but otherwise it remains somewhat featureless. Pevsner's assessment was lukewarm: *"Little survives by way of interior decoration, although the space remains impressive" (Bettley and Pevsner, 144)*. This is not unusual for re-used Adam buildings; indeed it has been said that *"few people have ever seen a really first class Adam building both inside and out" (ODNB)*.

The newly completed playhouse had an ornamented proscenium arch at the southern end (between the present pair of staircases), with a forestage and two proscenium doors, all elegantly decorated. The present cloakrooms on either side of the proscenium arch were probably the dressing rooms, while the cupboards and kitchen areas along the eastern and western sides may originally have housed the stairs to the upper boxes and gallery. The audience occupied the pit, two tiers of boxes and the gallery at the northern end of the theatre.

The theatre continued to be referred to as The New

Theatre' until at least 1780, but by 1793 it had become known simply as The Playhouse or The Theatre. It was until 1819 to remain the Bury home of the Norwich Company of Comedians, during the most celebrated and successful period in their history.

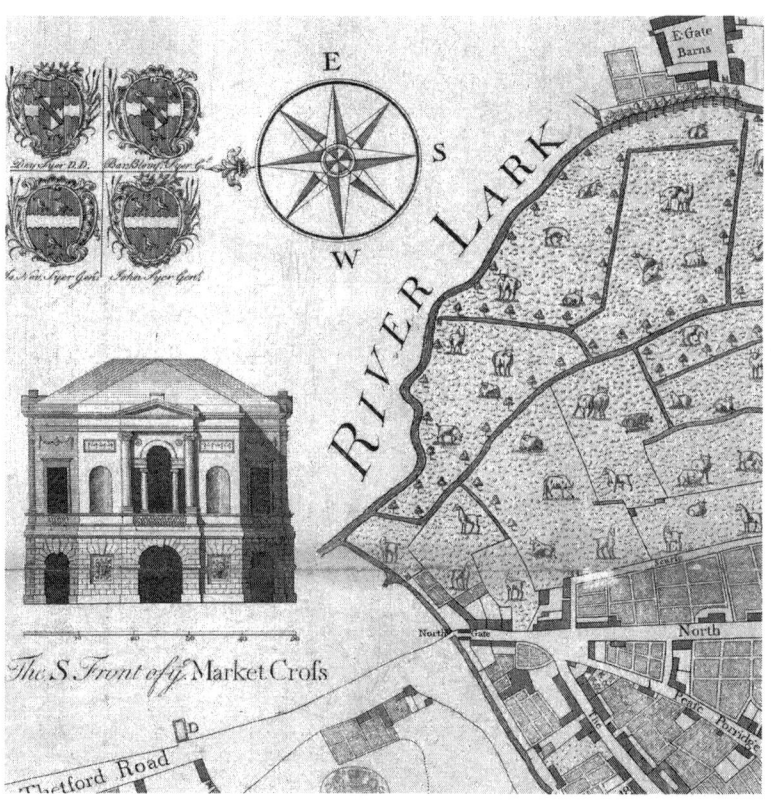

Adam's Market Cross, detail from Thomas Warren's 1776 map of Bury (Moyse's Hall Museum)

Positively the last Time of performing in TOWN this SEASON.

FOR THE YEARLY BENEFIT OF
Mr. and Mrs. SIMPSON.

By his *Majesty's Servants* from the *Theatre-Royal* in NORWICH,
At the THEATRE in BURY ST. EDMUND'S,
On SATURDAY, AUGUST the 8th, will be reviv'd a TRAGEDY, call'd,

Tancred and Sigismunda.

(Written by THOMPSON, Author of the SEASONS, &c.)

TANCRED, Mr. BRUNTON.
Earl OSMOND, Mr. POLLETT.
RODOLPHO, Mr. BANISTER.
First OFFICER, Mr. CORNELYS.
Second OFFICER, Mr. SIMPSON.
OFFICER to SIFFREDI, Mr. MILLER.
SIFFREDI, Mr. HOLLAND.

LAURA, Mrs. BANISTER.
SIGISMUNDA, Mrs. SIMPSON.

To which will be added a COMEDY of Three Acts, (never acted here,) call'd,

The COZENERS.

[Written by SAMUEL FOOTE, Esq;]
And perform'd at the THEATRE-ROYAL in the Hay-market, with universal Applause.

Mr. AIRCASTLE, Mr. HOLLAND.
PRIG, Mr. DANCER.
Colonel GORGET, Mr. POLLETT.
Mr. O'FLANNAGAN, Mr. CORNELYS.
FLAW, Mr. MILLER.
MOSES, MANASSES, Mr. MURRAY.
ROGER, Mr. CROUSE.
HELLEBORE, Mr. SIMPSON.
SERVANT, Mr. ROSS.
TOBY, Mr. BANISTER.

Mrs. FLEECE'EM, Mrs. IBBOTT.
BETSY BLOSSOM, Mrs. MURRAY.
MARIANNE, Mrs. DANCER.
MAID, Mrs. CROUSE.
Mrs. AIRCASTLE, Mrs. BANISTER.

To begin precisely at SEVEN o'Clock.———*Vivant Rex et Regina*
BOXES, 3s.———UPPER BOXES, 2s. 6d.———PIT, 2s. 6d.———GALLERY, 1s.

TICKETS to be had of Mr. and Mrs. SIMPSON; the *Angel, Grey-hound, Six-bells,* Mr. *Green's* Printing-office, and of Mr. *Beacham* at the THEATRE of whom Places may be taken from Ten to Twelve each Day.
N. B. No Places can be secur'd unless Tickets are taken at the same Time.

Playbill, 8 August 1778
(all playbills, Suffolk Archives)

THE NORWICH COMPANY OF COMEDIANS

THE NORWICH COMPANY of Comedians are first recorded as *"Servants to his Grace the Duke of Grafton"* (their first patron) in 1726. Two year later they appeared for the first time at the Bury Fair and, as we have seen, gave the opening performance of the first Bury Playhouse in 1734. By the time The New Theatre opened, they had become the resident company. *"His Majesty's Servants from the Theatre Royal In Norwich"* enjoyed a national reputation, and were described by Coleridge in 1794 as *"the first provincial Actors in the Kingdom"*.

The annual Norwich Theatrical Circuit covered Norwich and six outlying theatres, and became an established feature of the East Anglian social calendar. James Winston's 1805 account *The Theatric Tourist* described the circuit:

> The year is made out thus: first, Yarmouth, then Ipswich, (for the races) a distance of fifty-three miles; forty-three more to Norwich (for the Assizes); back to Yarmouth, twenty-two; then to Stirbitch [Stourbridge Fair, Cambridge], eighty-six; to Bury [for the

Fair], twenty-eight; Colchester, twenty-two; to Ipswich again (for Christmas), eighteen; to Norwich, forty-three; Lynn, forty-four; back again to Norwich, forty-four; and again to Yarmouth, twenty-two; making in the whole a very pretty twelvemonth tour.

Norwich was one of several theatrical circuits around the country (including Bath, Bristol, Edinburgh, Lincoln, Nottingham and York), but was considered one of the better circuits outside London.

Although theatre programmes did not appear until the Victorian period, the Norwich Company printed and distributed playbills to advertise their forthcoming productions. A small collection of these from the period 1776—1802 is held by Suffolk Archives in the Bury Record Office, and provides an insight into the performances, practices and personalities of the Norwich Company on their regular visits to the Bury Theatre.

The playbills display the ticket prices of the time. In the 1770s, the lower boxes cost 3/- (15p), the upper boxes and pit 2/6d (12.5p), and the gallery 1/- (5p). By the early 1800s, these prices had risen slightly, the lower boxes costing 4/- (20p), the upper boxes 3/- and the pit 2/6d. It was also possible to gain 'half-price' entry to the pit for 1/6d (7.5p), either for latecomers admitted after the second or third act or for those who chose to attend for only part of the evening. Given that the annual income for a working family in the 18th century was probably no more than £15 to £20, these prices would have been beyond the means of many. However, it must be remembered that the Bury Fair was the highlight of the local social calendar, and for many it would have provided the only theatrical entertainment of the year.

The division of the theatre into pit, boxes and gallery closely reflected the growing social divisions of the day. The two tiers of boxes were mainly occupied by the wealthy county set, who usually arrived in their own carriages, complete with a pair of postillions. They included the landed gentry, wealthy local farmers (after the harvest had been brought in) and the *nouveau-riche* businessmen and owners of the newly-built (or newly-Georgianised) townhouses of Georgian Bury.

One such businessman was wealthy yarn-maker, banker, Alderman and diarist James Oakes, 'Mr Bury St Edmunds'. Oakes was so successful that he was able to engage celebrated architect John Soane to redesign his fine Georgian townhouse in Guildhall Street. He was very active in Bury society, and it is clear from his diaries that he and his family (including his children and grandchildren from the age of nine) were regular visitors to the theatre *(Fiske 1990, 171)*. He would also present theatre tickets as gifts to his friends and occasionally to his clerks *(Fiske 1990, 357)*.

Performances at the theatre usually started at 6pm, so to ensure that the gentry were able to reserve their places, the playbills advised that *"Ladies and Gentlemen are requested to send Servants to keep their places by 5 o'clock"*. They often lasted until 11pm or midnight, and patrons were promised (or forewarned) that *"gentlemen and ladies at a distance would in their Return have the Opportunity of the Moon"* (Rosenfeld, *301)*.

Like the grand assemblies at 'The Assembly Rooms' (the Athenaeum), performances at the theatre were highly fashionable events, where it was important both to see and be seen. Mary Hanson, writing in 1779, noted that:

> Two nights are always good ones … for what fine folks we have in Town goe those nights and that brings numbers of other people to see them, so between seeing and to be seen there is a great number gathered together.
>
> *(Grice, 145)*

The pit was favoured by the emerging 'middling sort', by theatre devotees and by those young 'gallants', whose practice of sitting on the stage behind the scenery had been widespread until David Garrick's celebrated 'Banishment of the Beau' at Drury Lane in 1747. The Bury playbills followed suit by making it clear that *"No Gentlemen (in future) can be admitted behind the Scenes"*.

The gallery was generally reserved for the poorer theatregoers, the Georgian counterparts of Shakespeare's 'groundlings'. They might be eating oranges, smoking clay pipes or swigging from beer bottles, sometimes propositioning, often heckling the performance and even bombarding the actors with orange peel or nutshells if they didn't 'play to the gallery'. Both oranges and nuts were on sale every evening in the theatre, and an advertisement in the *Bury and Norwich Post* of October 1782 describing fruit seller Henry Fulcher's walnuts as *"the well-known High Flyers" (McCutcheon, 60)* suggests that they were more valued as missiles than refreshments.

*The Market Cross, c. 1700, unknown artist
(Moyse's Hall Museum)*

*Robert Adam, attributed to George Willison, c. 1770–74
(National Portrait Gallery 2953)*

*Adam's Market Cross, north elevation
(Brian Mawdsley/Historic England)*

Adam's Market Cross, west elevation

The Comedy panel (left), and Tragedy panel (right)

Detail of the Comedy panel, showing musical notes

Adam's Market Cross, interior

Pit Boxes and Gallery by George Cruickshank, 1834
(British Library)

Alderman's silver tickets (Moyse's Hall Museum)

Elizabeth Inchbald by Thomas Lawrence, 1796

Declaring the General Election results, 19 July 1895

The Market Cross Fire, March 1908

Town Hall postcard, 1914

Adam's Market Cross, south elevation

The unruly behaviour in the gallery would often spill over into other parts of the theatre. William Wilkins the Elder described the foyer of the Norwich Theatre in 1799:

> the entrances and exits being so ill-contrived that only one person can approach the Lobby, a Lady must be separated from the arm of her protector both on entering and leaving ... it is really otherwise impossible that Ladies can reach their carriages without danger of spoiling their dresses ... being squeezed perhaps between doorkeepers, porters and prostitutes who are forcing their way without regard to Beauty or Dress
>
> *(Miller, 18)*

Until 1780, tickets were available from the lodgings of the actor-managers or various members of the company. These included actor-managers William Crouse (at Mrs Griffin's, opposite the theatre), Richard Griffith (at Mr Royal's, in Whiting Street) and Mr Barrett (at the Bell Inn), or company members such as Mr and Mrs Dancer (at Mrs Jermyn's), Mr and Mrs Holland, Mr and Mrs Simpson, Mr Browne, or Mr and Mrs Bannister (at Mr Trevathan's). Tickets were later available from Mr Beacham at the Theatre, Mr Green's Printing Office and variously from The Angel, The Greyhound, The Six Bells and Anderson's Coffee House.

By 1793, the sale of tickets appears to have been centralised at the theatre, at first in the hands of Mr Bartram and, by 1802, Mr Stannard, when both tickets and playbills were being printed by Peter Gedge, printer of the *Bury and Norwich Post*.

The Alderman (or mayor) of the town was provided with a silver token, entitling him to unlimited free entry to the theatre. This privilege was later extended to theatre subscribers and shareholders, though there were frequent disputes about whether they were transferable to friends and family. Some examples of the Aldermen's tokens are held in Moyse's Hall Museum.

Today, without its boxes and gallery, it is hard to estimate the original capacity of the theatre. It would certainly have exceeded what would be considered safe by modern standards. Wilkins refers to it as 'the little theatre', so it was clearly smaller than other theatres in the Norwich Circuit. Its successor, the Theatre Royal, could accommodate 780 spectators, with 360 in the boxes, 300 in the pit and 120 in the gallery *(Grice, 143),* though its modern-day capacity is limited to only 360 in total.

Some indication of its capacity is provided by James Oakes' description of a visit to the theatre on Friday 19 October 1798:

> to the Play bespoke by the Military associations. The Pitt entirely fill'd by Lord Brome's Troop, Lord Hervey's Ickworth Troop, Lord Hervey's Bury Volunteers and Dr Ord's Village Association, abt 180 in the Pitt besides. The 2 upper Forms taken off for the female part of their Familys. The house

never known so full, should imagine nearly 70£House [£70 takings].

(Fiske 1990, 369)

Oakes' use of the word 'besides' implies that the pit accommodated a number greater than 180. Assuming a pit capacity of, say, 250 and based on the proportions of the Theatre Royal, this would suggest a total capacity of around 650. This seems high, even by the standards of the time. Still less likely is Oakes' estimate of £70 in ticket sales which, based on known ticket prices, would suggest an even higher capacity of around 750 – as many as the Theatre Royal, which was specifically designed to hold more. If instead we take Oakes' estimate of 180 to include all those in the pit, this suggests a total capacity of around 450, which seems a more realistic estimate.

'Bespoke' performances were one of the most lucrative sources of income for the company. Local landowners, businesses, army regiments, and even licensing magistrates could 'bespeak' a performance by subsidising it, or more commonly, by prebooking all or part of the theatre.

It was customary for the Alderman to choose a play to be performed during the Bury Fair, and in return he was obliged to buy a large number of tickets. On Saturday 22 October 1785, for example, James Oakes attended 'The Alderman and Corporation Play', Elizabeth Inchbald's new comedy *I'll tell you what*, and he notes that "*The Box's in general very full, a thin Pitt. The play universally admired*" (Fiske 1990, 240).

On Monday 2 Nov 1802, he attended:

> My bespoke play as Alderman & for the Corporation: The Gamester & Ways & Means. I bot 30 Tickets ... The Boxes well filld, the Pitt not altogether so. Almost the whole of the Corporation & Trades people of the Town, very few of the principal Ladys & Gentn. An extremely deep Tragedy – the Farce laughable enough.
>
> *(Fiske 1991, 31)*

Wealthy local landowners such as the Herveys of Ickworth regularly bespoke plays. On Thursday Oct 25 1804, for example, Oakes attended:

> Lord & Lady Bristols' Play this Eveng (The Rivals & the Critick). We all went & had the stage Box opposite Lord Bristol's ... I did not go till just [as?] the Entertainment was beginning.
>
> *(Fiske 1991, 59)*

The plays would have been chosen by the Herveys, and they would have bought a considerable number of tickets for the performance.

Army regiments also bespoke plays at the theatre. On Monday 28 October 1793, a bespoke performance of Centlivre's 1714 comedy *The Wonder! A Woman Keeps a Secret* and O'Keefe's 1786 comic opera *Patrick in Prussia, or Love in a Camp* was performed "*By Desire of the Officers of the West Kent Regiment*".

By DESIRE of the OFFICERS of the
WEST KENT REGIMENT.

On MONDAY, October 28, 1793,

Will be performed the Comedy of

The WONDER!

A Woman keeps a Secret.

Don Felix, by Mr. POWELL,
Liffardo, Mr. DEATH—Gibby, Mr. WHITE,
Don Pedro, Mr. JACKSON—Don Lopez, Mr. MORETON,
Frederick, Mr. J. BENNETT,
And Colonel Briton, by Mr. SEYMOUR.

Flora, by Mrs. POWELL,
Ifabella, Mrs. TOWNSEND—Inis, Mrs. ÆCEY,
And Violante, by Mifs EDMEAD.

End of the Play,
A DOUBLE HORNPIPE,
By Mr. J. BENNETT and Mrs. CHESNUT.

To which will be added, the Mufical Entertainment of

Patrick in Pruffia.

Darby, Mr. WADDY,
Olmutz, Mr. BENNETT—Father Luke, Mr. TUTHILL,
Quiz, Mr. JACKSON—Marfhall, Mr. WHITE,
Rupert, Mr. J. BENNETT,
And Patrick, by Mr. TOWNSEND.

Flora, by Mifs WILKINSON,
Mabel Flourifh, Mrs. ÆCEY,
And Norah, by Mrs. TAYLOR.

☞ By Permiffion of the Commanding Officer, the REGIMENTAL BAND will perform in the Orcheftra.

⁎ To begin exactly at Half paft Six o'Clock.——Boxes 3s.—Pit 2s. 6d.—Gallery 1s.

By DESIRE of the GENTLEMEN of the GRAMMAR SCHOOL,
To-morrow, The INCONSTANT,
With The PRISONER at LARGE.
BEING THE LAST NIGHT BUT ONE OF PERFORMING.

The West Kent Militia was one of a number of non-Suffolk regiments billeted locally during the French Revolution (1789—99). The strong military presence in Bury during this period was marked by occasional regimental concerts at the theatre. In October 1793, for example, there was a concert by the band of the West Kent Regiment, and in September 1796 by the New Romney Fencible Regiment Band *(Fiske 1990, 336)*.

Outside the Bury Fair season, the theatre occasionally provided other forms of entertainment. On Friday 9 March 1804, Oakes records that *"Mr & Mrs Baker all went to the Theatre to hear Incleton, the great Singer" (Fiske 1991, 52)*. Charles Benjamin Incledon was a Cornish tenor, who became one of the foremost English singers of his day.

On Friday 26 June 1807 Oakes' family *"went to hear Banister deliver his Budget at the Theatre from 8 to ten o'clock"*. Jack Bannister was an actor who performed a musical monologue called 'Bannister's Budget' and delighted the audience with *"the versatility of his comic and mimic talents" (Fiske 1991, 96)*.

DESPITE ITS COMPARATIVELY small size, the Bury Theatre was commercially successful, and indeed helped subsidise other, less lucrative, theatres on the circuit. Its popularity was such that the company sometimes backtracked to Bury for bespoke performances, a distinction shared only with the Norwich Theatre. Box office receipts for the 1771 summer circuit, which in that year included Woodbridge, Norwich, Colchester and Bury, amounted to a respectable £2,734.

However, business was not always as good. 1774 proved

a lean year for the company, as the famous London clown Lewy Owen played in Bury to packed houses. Actor-manager Richard Griffith complained bitterly:

> No wonder that theft and drunkenness and distress so abound when people go to booths instead of theatres, and prefer seeing a mountebank stand on his head, to an able tragedian in the character of Hamlet.
>
> *(Grice, 145)*

There were also occasionally other theatrical attractions in Bury. In January 1784, "*a Company of Gentlemen ... for the benefit of the poor of this Town*" presented *Orphans of China*, *Venice Preserv'd* and *The Minor* at the Assembly Room (the Athenaeum). The following year they presented *The Royal Convert* and *The Minor* at the same venue. These productions took place outside the Bury Fair season, often to raise money for the poor in times of hardship (winters were particularly harsh in the mid-1780s), and were not intended to rival the Norwich Company.

The repertoire of the Norwich Circuit was wide, and may have extended to 40 to 50 works at any one time *(Mackintosh 1979, 24)*. These included Shakespearean and other Elizabethan tragedies, Restoration Comedies and new pieces. A typical programme would include a main piece, either a comedy or tragedy or a recent success in London or Cambridge, followed by an 'afterpiece' – a farce, musical interlude ('*burletta*'), pantomime or a ballad opera in the style of *The Beggar's Opera*. Shakespearean tragedies were the most frequently-performed pieces, with Macbeth a particular favourite. However, some of these were probably 'improved' (or abridged) versions of the full play, such as *King Lear* on Saturday 26 October 1793, which was preceded by Pearce's new two-act comic opera *Midnight Wanderers* and concluded with a double hornpipe by Mr Bennet and Mrs Chesnut.

In the company's early days, last-minute programme changes were quite common, so that audiences might arrive expecting to see one play and find the curtain rising on another. However, this practice was unpopular with audiences, and occurred less frequently as the company's reputation grew *(Rosenfeld, 302)*.

The company had its own stock scenery and sets (such as a street scene, palace, forest or prison), which were stored and repainted in its Norwich workshop during the winter. Apart from the actor-manager, the scenic artist was the most highly paid member of any company and some, such as the French-Italian John Devoto (active 1708—52), became nationally famous. The company also employed decorators and carpenters, and spent some £25 each year on paint alone. Some of the larger theatres also had their own stock scenery and wings, which were changed in full view of the audience, either by a rope and pulley system or by using the 'book' principle, rather like a rotating display stand.

Various types of machinery were used to provide special effects, such as wave, thunder and wind machines, and devices for 'flyings' and 'sinkings'. Trapdoors were used where the stage allowed; on one occasion in Norwich:

> a trap-door opened, and four of the company

> fell in – one a particular man, who was high-sheriff last year, fell upon a pretty woman, and liked his situation so well, that they could not get him out
>
> *(Rosenfeld, 290)*

The company prided itself on its costumes, often referred to as its 'proper decorations' or 'habits'. Women were often expected to provide their own wardrobe of costumes for all types of production, though the company engaged a hairdresser in each town to curl the gentlemen's hair and keep the wigs in order.

Theatre lighting was provided by oil lamps, and by candles on the front of the boxes and in the footlights, creating a smoky and probably noxious atmosphere. Indeed the expression 'smelling the lamp' became a euphemism for acting. Despite this, the theatres seemed to have remained chilly, and several of the 1793 playbills reassured theatregoers that '*Constant fires are kept in the theatre*'.

Scenery, costumes and props were conveyed around the theatre circuit in a convoy of 3 to 6 six-ton wagons, each drawn by six horses. Actors, musicians and crew (including stage-keepers, property men, lamplighters and billstickers) walked at the rear of the convoy, though senior members might be allowed to share a chaise. The convoy was often met on the outskirts of town by excited groups of children, and triumphally entered the town to a riotous welcome. In smaller towns, it was the highlight of the year.

The company usually numbered 15 to 25 at any one time, and particularly favoured employing married couples, to save money on wages. Regular performers included the Bannisters (plus the young Miss Bannister), Bowmans, Browns, Chambers, Chesnuts, Crouses, Dancers, Fitzgeralds, Hollands (who had a 20-year association with the company), Lassells (plus the young Miss Lassells), Millers, Powells, Rosses, Simpsons, Tuthills and Whites. Productions would often include two (or even three) members of the same family. However men always received top billing even when, as in the production of *Jane Shore* in October 1780, Mrs Simpson was playing the title role.

Actors were normally paid a wage of between £1 and 30s per week, though the actor-manager would receive more. In addition, each actor was usually awarded one benefit performance a year, giving them all the box office takings, which might amount to as much as £40. For example, on 6 November 1779, James Oakes attended a performance for the benefit of an actor in gaol *(Fiske 1990, 214),* and on 19 October 1784 a performance for the benefit of actor-manager Giles Barrett *(Fiske 1990, 235).* Actors were usually employed on a 3-year contract, with a £500 forfeiture for early termination. This was a relatively privileged position compared to many other companies, who paid their actors on an iniquitous profit-share basis.

However working conditions were demanding; every day, actors were expected to learn 500 lines, attend four hours of rehearsal and perform for up to five hours. They also needed to be versatile, capable of performing tragedy, comedy, music and dance as each production required. They were assisted in this by a strict convention of type-casting; male actors might be hired as First or Second Tragedian, First or Second

'Heavy Man' (villain), First or Second Low Comedian, First or Second Old Man, or Walking Gentleman, while female actors might be hired as First Tragedy Lady, First Comedy Lady, First or Second Singing Lady, Old Woman, and so on *(Miller, 24)*.

BY HIS MAJESTY's SERVANTS,
From the THEATRE-ROYAL, in NORWICH.

At the New THEATRE, in BURY ST. EDMUND's,
On FRIDAY October 20, 1780, will be presented a TRAGEDY, called

JANE SHORE.

(By NICHOLAS ROWE, Esq;)

Lord HASTINGS by Mr. BARRETT
Duke of GLOSTER by Mr. MURRAY
Earl of DERBY by Mr. CROUSE
CATESBY by Mr. SIMPSON
RADCLIFFE by Mr. DANCER
BELMOUR by Mr. MILLER
PORTER by Mr. WILLIAMS
And DUMONT by Mr. POLLETT

ALICIA by Mrs. MILLER
MAIDS to ALICIA, Mrs. CROUSE, and Mrs. HOLLAND,
And JANE SHORE by Mrs. SIMPSON

SINGING, by Mrs. WESTON

To which will be added a Celebrated Burletta (performed here but once) called,

POOR VULCAN.

With New Scenery and Decorations.
The MUSIC composed and compiled by Mr. DIBDIN.
The PAINTINGS by Mr. WESTON

VULCAN,⎫ ⎧ *Crump*, Mr. DANCER
MARS, ⎪ ⎪ *Pike*, Mr. BANISTER
BACCHUS, ⎬ ALIAS ⎨ *Gauge*, Mr. DAVIS
ADONIS, ⎪ ⎪ *Joe*, Mr. MILLER
And JUPITER,⎭ ⎩ *Stud*, Mr. BROWNE

GRACE by Mrs- ROSS
And VENUS, alias MAUDLIN, Mrs. WESTON

———To begin exactly at SIX o'Clock.——— *Vivant Rex et Regina*.
BOXES, 3s.——UPPER BOXES, 2s. 6d.——PIT, 2s. 6d.——GALLERY, 1s.
N. B. No PLACES can be secured, unless TICKETS are taken at the same Time.
414 Nothing less then the WHOLE, and HALF-PRICE will be taken at the PIT End, during the Time of Performance.
TICKETS to be had of Mr. BARRETT, at the BELL INN; of Mr. CROUSE, opposite the THEATRE; at ANDERSON's COFFEE-HOUSE, and GREEN's PRINTING-OFFICE.
N. B. No Gentlemen (in future) can be admitted behind the Scenes

Giles Barrett as Charles Surface in 'School for Scandal'
(Victoria and Albert Museum)

Reviews of the company's productions were generally favourable, though not always so. In October 1783, for example, newly arrived from Stourbridge Fair, the company opened with a performance of the tragedy *Isabella*, on which the Theatrical Register of the *Bury and Norwich Post* of 8 October observed that *"the fatigue of the journey had to some degree impaired the memory"*.

Three days later, the same observer said of Mr Bowles

that he *"had given a fair performance, but was exhorted by our critic to look at the person to whom he was speaking, and not fix his eyes upon the audience as though to court applause"*.

And on 13 October the incensed critic wrote of the company's pantomime *Harlequin's Trip to Bury* that:

> it is a species of entertainment too despicable for criticism; and though custom has long sanctioned it in obedience to the depraved state of the rabble, it is an insult to a rational British audience.
>
> (McCutcheon, 63)

WE KNOW RELATIVELY little of the lives or personalities of members of the company. However, there are a few exceptions.

Richard Griffith was actor-manager of the Norwich Company throughout the rebuilding of the Bury Theatre, from 1766—80. He was an actor of the old school: naive, pleasure-loving and vain, he was keen on fishing and shooting and, although popular, was the butt of numerous practical jokes by his fellow actors. He was responsible for introducing many new plays direct from their London premieres, and was said to have inspired the young Elizabeth Inchbald's love of the theatre.

Giles Linnett Barrett succeeded Griffith as actor-manager from 1780—88, and appears in a number of 1780 Bury playbills. He was by all accounts a competent, though not brilliant, actor. It was under his management that the Norwich Circuit was extended in 1782 to include Stourbridge Fair in

Cambridge, and in 1788 he persuaded the celebrated actress Sarah Siddons to play eight roles in nine nights at Norwich, all opposite him. He later left his wife and travelled to the newly independent United States, where he achieved some success on the stages of Boston and New York.

John Brunton as Altamont in 'The Fair Penitent', 1806 (Illinois Library Digital Collections)

John Brunton succeeded Barrett as actor-manager in 1788, and appears in several Bury playbills from 1778—93. He was a talented, popular and generous veteran actor, described by contemporaries as:

> 'our leading tragedian and one of the best Shylocks I have ever seen' and 'a prince among actor-managers'
>
> *(Grice, 74)*

His 11-year tenure as actor-manager marked the most successful and confident decade in the history of the Norwich Company. In 1791 he established the Norwich Theatrical Fund to support sick and retired company actors, the first of its kind in the country. Three of his daughters, Anne, Elizabeth and Louisa, became successful actresses, one of whom appears as Miss Brunton in a Bury playbill of 1793. Brunton was succeeded as lessee of the circuit in 1799 by William Wilkins Senior, whose son was to design and build Bury's 'New Theatre' (or Theatre Royal) in 1819.

Elizabeth Inchbald was an actress and writer closely associated with the Norwich Company. She was probably the greatest English female dramatist of the 18th century. Born Elizabeth Simpson, at Stanningfield near Bury in 1753, as a girl she was a frequent visitor to the Market Cross Playhouse, apparently due to a deep infatuation with actor-manager Richard Griffith. Her brother George joined the Norwich Company in 1770, and appears with Mrs Simpson (presumably his wife) in several of the Bury playbills.

Elizabeth, however, ran away to London at eighteen, where she married Joseph Inchbald, an actor twice her age. Here, as well as acting, she wrote many successful comedies, farces and sentimental dramas, some of which (such as *The Wedding Day*) were considered highly risqué. As well as being a talented writer and radical thinker, she was also a famous beauty, referred to by actor-manager Tate Wilkinson as 'The Lovely Inchbald' whose admirers included such prominent figures as Richard Sheridan, John Kemble and Charles Lamb. A number of her plays were performed at the Bury Theatre, including the socially-liberal *Everyone has his Fault* in October 1793.

THEATRE, BURY.

On SATURDAY, OCTOBER 12, 1793,
(Never performed here) a COMEDY called

Every one has his Fault.

Sir Robert Ramble, by Mr. POWELL,
Mr. Irwin, Mr. SEYMOUR,
Lord Norland, Mr. BENNETT,
Mr. Placid, Mr. DEATH----Mr. Harmony, Mr. WHITE,
Edward, Miſs JACKSON,
Hammond, Mr. CHESNUT----Porter, Mr. TUTHILL,
And Mr. Solus, by Mr. FOOTE.
Miſs Wooburn, by Mrs. TAYLOR,
Mrs. Placid, Mrs. POWELL,
Miſs Spinſter, Mrs. ÆCEY,
And Lady Eleanor Irwin, by Miſs EDMEAD.

End of the Play, a New Dance, called
The SAILOR's RETURN,
By Mr. J. BENNETT and Mrs. CHESNUT.

To which will be added, the Muſical Entertainment of

The Flitch of Bacon.

Major Benbow, by Mr. WHITE,
Captain Greville, Mr. TOWNSEND,
Juſtice Benbow, Mr. FOOTE,
Tipple, Mr. JACKSON,
Captain Wilſon, by Mr. BENNETT.
And Eliza, by Mrs. TAYLOR.

*** To begin exactly at Half paſt Six o'Clock.——Boxes 3s.—Pit 2s. 6d.—Gallery 1s.
Tickets and Places for the Boxes may be had of Mr. BARTRAM, at the Theatre, from Eleven till One o'Clock.
Places cannot be ſecured unleſs Tickets are taken.—No Admiſſion behind the Scenes.
☞ Ladies and Gentlemen are requeſted to ſend Servants to keep their Places by Five o'Clock.

On MONDAY,
ALEXANDER the GREAT,
With (Firſt Time) a Grand Ballet Pantomime called
OSCAR and MALVINA.

Samuel Foote as Fondlewife in 'The Old Bachelor', 1776

Samuel Foote, 'the English Aristophanes', was an actor-manager, dramatist and satirist, and a favourite of the Norwich Company repertoire. A former owner of the Haymarket Theatre, his comedies feature regularly in the Bury playbills, including *Piety in Pattens or the Virtuous Housemaid* (performed in August 1776), *The Author* (July 1778), *The Devil Upon Two Sticks* and *The Cozeners* (August 1778) and *The Lyar* (October 1793).

Sarah Ibbott was one of the Norwich Company's leading actresses, featuring in several of the Bury playbills, including the principal role of Mrs Malaprop in Sheridan's *The Rivals* in October 1780. She was apparently rather plump, with actor-manager Tate Wilkinson unkindly comparing her with her predecessor, Mrs Baker:

> good voice, education, and understanding – not equal in expression to Mrs Baker; her manner far from accomplished: however, if size was necessary, though Mrs Baker was not a skeleton, yet Ibbott made more than treble amends as to the quantity.
>
> *(Grice, 55)*

It was said at the time that, had she been prettier, she would have been a darling of the London stage.

Elizabeth 'Eliza' O'Neill was a celebrated Irish actress, who appeared as a guest of the company in one of the last productions ever to be staged at the Market Cross theatre. On Friday 16 October 1818, James Oakes wrote:

> At home till 1/2 past 6 o'clock then went to the Theatre to the Play, Venice Preserv'd to see Miss Neill act the part of Belvidera. We returnd home as soon as the Play was over. The House most remarkably full, 1/2 Pitt taking into Boxs. Box price 6/-, pitt 4/-, Gallery 1/6.
>
> *(Fiske 1991, 232)*

Eliza O'Neill's appearance represented quite a coup for

the company, which took the opportunity to raise its ticket prices. She was famous both for her tragic roles as Juliet and Belvidera and for her great beauty, which was said to have caused men to be borne fainting from the theatre.

Eliza O'Neill by Henry Hoppner Meyer, c. 1820
(National Library of Wales)

WILLIAM WILKINS AND THE BURY NEW THEATRE

THE WEALTHY WILKINS family of Norwich had been shareholders in the company since 1768, but were soon destined to play a more prominent role in its history. In 1799, impresario and ornamental plasterer William Wilkins the Elder leased the entire Norwich Circuit for seven years, at an annual rental of £750. His offer for the circuit was accepted after former actor-manager John Brunton withdrew a rival bid.

The lease included the annual rental of the Bury Theatre for £130 – a substantial increase on its annual rent of £42 in 1734 and £80 in 1779, reflecting the rising stock of the company. The lease for the theatre was awarded on condition that only the Norwich Company should perform there, and then only for a maximum of six weeks a year *(Fiske 1990, 381)*.

In 1808, William Wilkins the Younger took over the lease of the Bury Theatre from his father. Already a successful neoclassical architect, having designed Downing College, Cambridge and Nelson's Pillar in Dublin, Wilkins would later go on to design the National Gallery and University

College, London.

On the death of his father in 1815, Wilkins inherited the entire Norwich Circuit of theatres, and continued to manage them for the rest of his life. During this time he rebuilt or remodelled several of the theatres, and occasionally even designed scenery. Under both father and son, actor-managers of the company were appointed as sub-lessees.

Wilkins soon realised the limitations of the Bury Theatre. It was cramped (the smallest of the Norwich Circuit theatres) but its season was one of the most successful on the circuit, and was often used to subsidise the less profitable theatres. As Wilkins himself acknowledged:

> At Bury, in the piping times of war, the little theatre was one of the most productive and the most inconvenient in the circuit, and I was naturally stimulated to render it more worthy of the town of Bury and its important neighbourhood.
>
> *(Grice, 148)*

Wilkins raised his concerns with the corporation, who had already established a committee in 1806 *"to examine the state and condition of the shops and cellars in and under the Market Cross in this Borough and what they are worth to be let"*. They offered Wilkins use of the Guildhall as a replacement for the Theatre, but he dismissed the idea, claiming that the building (now Grade I Listed) was only fit for demolition.

Eventually, on 7 November 1818, Wilkins persuaded the corporation to agree that he could build elsewhere a *"theatre *of ample dimensions and elegance corresponding to the other public buildings of the place"* (Mackintosh 1979, 16). It was agreed that he would pay the corporation an annual rental of £20, in exchange for an exclusive licence to present theatrical performances in Bury.

Soon afterwards, Wilkins informed the corporation that he had '*purchased a piece of ground in Westgate Street*' for this purpose, for a sum of £200. It was a semi-rural, sloping site on the southern edge of the town. Although initially considered by theatre-goers as too far 'out of town', the sloping site was an architectural advantage to Wilkins. It enabled him to use the model of classical hillside theatres, such as Taormina in Sicily, to provide saloon-level entry to the boxes, while accommodating the pit, backstage and substage further down the slope.

The New Theatre was built at a cost of £5,000 (some £1,000 over budget), with the aid of £100 donations from each of 36 local subscribers, including James, Orbell and Henry Oakes *(Fiske 1991, 315n)*. It opened on Monday 11 October 1819 with George Colman's comedy *John Bull* and Thomas Morton's farce *A Roland for an Oliver*.

Its opening marked the end of an era for the old theatre, which turned its attention to other forms of popular entertainment. Within a few years the New Theatre had become known simply as 'The Theatre', until in 1845 its lessee William Abingdon renamed it 'The Theatre Royal', without any royal patent or authority to do so.

By that date the Norwich Circuit itself had disbanded, mainly for financial reasons. Wilkins had referred in 1831 to "*the depressed and ruinous state of Provincial Theatricals*", which he blamed on the influence of religious sectarians. However, its decline was accelerated by the arrival of the railways and by changing social tastes. Bury audiences could now seek their entertainment elsewhere, while those who remained behind were less devoted to the traditional repertoire of the Georgian stage, preferring instead such spectacles as Monsieur Gouffe who, in 1828 as *Jocko, the Brazilian Ape*, would:

> make a Descent from the Gallery to the Stage, suspended only by Three Fingers, and holding Two Flags ... and a 2nd Descent, Suspended by his Neck, Supporting a Boy and Waving Two Flags
>
> *(Miller, 36)*

The Theatre Royal, Bury St Edmunds

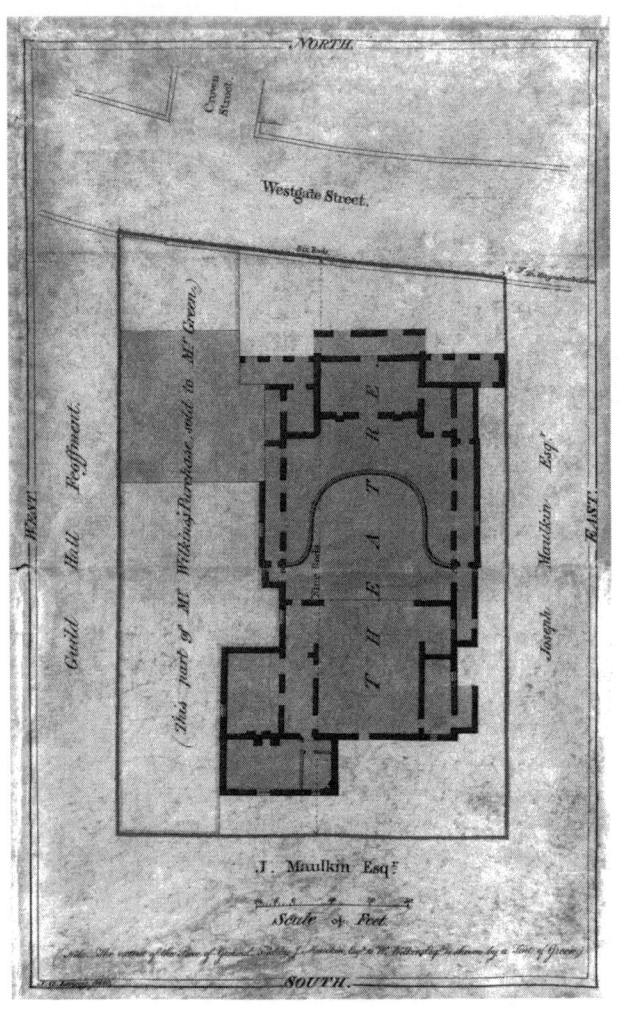

*Theatre Royal Deed-plan, J G Lenny 1818
(Suffolk Archives)*

THE VICTORIAN CONCERT ROOM AND TOWN HALL

IN RETURN FOR permission to build the New Theatre, the corporation required William Wilkins to convert the Market Cross Theatre into a 'public room', at his own expense. He did so, at a personal cost of £300, on condition that it would no longer be used for theatrical performance. He then removed:

> the stage, box front, seats, etc, many of which were renewed by Mr Wilkins when the lease was granted, together with the traps, machinery, wings, etc.
>
> *(Mackintosh 1979, 16)*

It appears that the theatre galleries remained in place, however, and were not removed until the building was damaged by fire nearly a century later.

On Thursday 27 May 1819, the corporation took over management of the upper floor of the Market Cross Theatre as a 'Concert Room'. This was a forerunner of the Victorian Music Hall, in which musical entertainment was mixed with comedy, speciality acts and variety.

One of the earliest events to be staged in the Concert Room was an exhibition of wax sculptures by the celebrated French artist Anna Maria 'Marie' Tussaud. She had exhibited once before in Bury and returned for the 1825 fair.

Imprisoned as a royalist during the French Revolution, she had later been employed to model the death masks of such prominent figures as Louis XVI, Marie Antoinette, Robespierre and Jean-Paul Marat. She came to England in 1802 and spent the next three decades touring the country with her collection, before setting up her permanent exhibition in Baker Street, London.

Madame Tussaud

The 1825 exhibition was advertised as *"a splendid promenade with magnificent coronation groups"*. Entry cost one shilling, and in the evenings the event was accompanied by a military band. The *Bury and Norwich Post* of Wednesday 5 October enthusiastically reported that:

> Madame Tussaud's Exhibition and Promenade is now open to the public, and we doubt not, from the very great improvement which this ingenious artiste has made in her collection, that it will again become, as upon its first visit, a subject of general attention, particularly during the approaching Fair, when it will doubtless be visited by every one possessing any taste for the fine arts.

It did indeed prove highly popular, becoming the 'must see' event of the year for the county set, while local parents were encouraged to take their children to visit the exhibition for its educational value.

In 1835, the Municipal Corporations Act replaced the old Bury Corporation with a new Bury St Edmunds Borough Council as owners of the Market Cross. At this time the council's list of tenants and annual rentals included Samuel Frost (£2 per year), Samuel Walliker (2 Guineas per year), S Fenton (3 Guineas per year) and Miss Grayston (cellar, 2 Guineas per year), while rental of the Concert Room was estimated at £12 per year.

The ground floor of the Market Cross continued to serve as the town's corn exchange until the 1830s. The council then decided that, like its commercial competitors elsewhere in East Anglia, Bury needed its own purpose-built corn exchange. The new building, opened on 4 January 1837, stood on an island site (now occupied by shops and a tearoom) immediately to the south of the Market Cross. It was built in similar neoclassical style, although of inferior quality and design *(Orbell 2017, 8)*.

It proved so commercially successful that it was extended in 1847 and eventually replaced in 1862 by the grand neoclassical third corn exchange, on an island site still further south, facing Abbeygate Street. This had been the site of the medieval butchers' shambles, and was earmarked for a covered provisions market in the 1850s, which was never built *(Orbell 2021)*. It is now occupied by shop units and a Wetherspoon's pub.

MEANWHILE, THE CONCERT Room continued to attract some of the most popular names of the day. Austrian concert pianist and composer Sigismond Thalberg, a contemporary and rival of Liszt, performed in the Concert Room in October 1837. The *Bury and Norwich Post* of 25 October described his concert in Bury as:

> The opportunity of hearing perhaps the first performer in the world … and his power and genius derive an additional charm from his gentlemanly and unassuming deportment.

It was received with applause which was *"literally tumultuous"*.

Chopin was less enthusiastic after hearing Thalberg play in Vienna when he wrote:

He plays splendidly, but he's not my man. He's younger than I, pleases the ladies … and wears diamond shirt studs.

On 27 July 1840, the council approved plans by Ipswich architect Benjamin Backhouse to create a Town Hall befitting its new proprietors. This was done by enclosing the ground floor, converting the north end of the upper storey into a reading room, altering the staircase, rebuilding the roof and removing the palisade erected in 1779. The trophy panels on the south side were replaced with sash windows, though were later reinstated. In November of that year the council resolved that the building *"heretofore known as the Market Cross shall in future be called the Town Hall"*.

A Liszt concert, cartoon by Theodor Hosemann, 1842

ON SATURDAY 19 September 1840, the famous Hungarian concert pianist and composer Franz Liszt appeared in the Concert Room as part of Louis Lavenu's six-week concert party tour. This was at the height of 'Lisztomania', when the handsome and charismatic performer provoked scenes of hysteria and 'swooning' among a legion of ecstatic female fans. They would avidly collect memorabilia of his performances, including discarded handkerchiefs, gloves, locks of hair, piano strings, coffee dregs and even discarded cigars:

> Liszt once threw away an old cigar stump in the street under the watchful eyes of an infatuated lady-in-waiting, who reverently picked the offensive weed out of the gutter, had it encased in a locket and surrounded with the monogram 'FL' in diamonds, and went about her courtly duties unaware of the sickly odour it gave forth.
>
> *(Walker, 372)*

Supporting Liszt on the tour was John Orlando Parry, an English pianist, baritone, actor and comic songwriter. As well as being a skilled accompanist, he wrote and performed burlesque songs, ballads, sketches and monologues, interspersed with impersonations of famous singers and quickfire costume-changes.

The *Bury and Norwich Post* of Wednesday 23 September judged Liszt's pianoforte playing '*wonderful*', but was less enthusiastic about Parry's performance:

Mr Parry was as happy as usual in his imitations and his Italian playing music though labouring under hoarseness in the evening; but the public have grown rather tired of these performances in a concert room.

John Orlando Parry, c. 1870
(National Library of Wales)

Throughout this period, the council had been working with the Eastern Union Railway Company on a historic change for the town: the proposed new Bury and Ipswich Railway. This led to one of the Town Hall's greatest civic occasions, the official opening of the new railway on Monday 7 December 1846, when it hosted a banquet for 300 passengers on the first train arriving at Bury's Northgate Station.

John Sims Reeves, 1889

A regular favourite in the Concert Room was operatic, oratorio and ballad tenor John Sims-Reeves. He became Britain's leading tenor, performing privately for Queen Victoria and Prince Albert, and having the popular song *Come into the Garden, Maud* written especially for him. He appeared in the Concert Room in September 1847, when the *Bury and Norwich Post* reported that:

> The general character of the selection was too dramatic for a concert-room, including

several pieces of that licentious description, which those who avoid the theatres cannot consistently tolerate.

However it goes on to concede that:

The attendance at the Concert was numerous and highly genteel, including nearly all the first families of the neighbourhood.

On this occasion, Sims-Reeves was accompanied by young Italian contralto Marietta Alboni, who went on to become one of the greatest contraltos in operatic history, and famously sang at the funeral of her mentor Rossini in 1868. The *Bury and Norwich Post* regarded her:

In the highest rank, undoubtedly … who though just past the [legal] age of womanhood, and labouring under the disadvantage of a figure embonpoint, 'and something more' took the town by surprise last season, and has in some measure divided public favour with the Swedish Nightingale [Jenny Lind].

Variety and novelty acts were also popular, and a foretaste of those which were to become the staple diet of late Victorian and Edwardian Music Halls. They included Swiss guitarist, concertina virtuoso and composer Giulio Regondi, a child prodigy who gave his first public guitar performance in London at the age of nine.

The Distin Family brass quintet appeared several times in the Concert Room. It consisted of John Distin and his four sons, playing trumpet, horn, cornet, bugle and trombone. They later adopted the newly-invented saxhorn, and performed privately for Queen Victoria and Prince Albert at Stowe House. One of their appearances in Bury was on Wednesday 19 March 1852 when, according to the *Bury and Norwich Post* of 26 March, "*there was a highly respectable attendance and the whole of the music was so well received*" and "*honoured with a rapturous encore.*"

The Distin Family, 1845

English stonemason and musician Joseph Richardson and his three sons performed at Bury in the 1840s on his patent 'lithophone'. This was made of Cumbrian whinstone, polished steel bars and Swiss bells, struck with small leather-covered wooden mallets. They played mainly opera and ballads and became hugely popular, touring the UK and Europe as 'Richardson & Sons, Rock, Bell and Steel Band'. They were particularly popular with the social elite, and performed by royal command for Queen Victoria at Buckingham Palace in February 1848.

Joseph Richardson and Sons, Buckingham Palace, 23 February 1848 (Keswick Museum & Art Gallery CC BY-SA 4.0)

Following this, The *Bury and Norwich Post* carried an announcement on Wednesday 6 September 1848:

> The Messieurs Richardson beg respectfully to announce that a grand morning and evening concert will be given … when the

Programmes will combine the same Pieces as selected by the Queen, and performed at the Soirées musicales at Buckingham Palace, in February last.

The tour included a concert at Bury on Friday 8 September 1848. Tickets for the morning concert (at 2pm) were 2/6d for adults, 1/- for children and schools, and 10/6d for families of up to five. Tickets for the 8pm evening concert were 2/- for reserved seats, 1/- for children and schools, and 1/- for back seats.

This was not their first visit to Bury, as the *Bury and Norwich Post* of 30 August had reminded its readers:

> Our readers no doubt remember the extraordinary 'concord of sweet sounds' presented to them a few years since by Messrs Richardson's ROCK band. It will be seen that they are about to repeat their visit, and that to the sonorous rock they have now added the metallic tones of the Chinese Steel Band and the Swiss bells, with that finest of all instruments, the human voice, in the person of Miss Julia Gould.

Among the regular performers of concert opera were the celebrated Italian soprano Giulia Grisi and her aristocratic husband Giovani Matteo di Candia ('Mario the Tenor'), who performed in Bury both individually and together. A glamorous celebrity couple who performed for the crowned heads of Europe, the principal roles of Norina and Ernesto in Donizetti's *Don Pasquale* had been created especially for them.

When they returned to perform together in October 1864, the *Bury and Norwich Post* of Tuesday 11 October reported that they would be performing "*a grand morning concert*", though not in the Concert Room but at the Athenaeum. The Athenaeum had been successful in attracting some eminent names from the worlds of literature (such as Dickens and Thackeray) and science (such as Astronomer Royal, George Biddell Airy). The Athenaeum also boasted a significantly larger capacity, and was perhaps beginning to supplant the Concert Room as Bury's principal musical entertainment venue. Was history repeating itself, and a building which had once been deemed too limiting as a theatre was now proving similarly restrictive as a music venue?

Giulia Grisi and Mario in Donizetti's Lucrezia Borgia, 1840

THE TOWN HALL continued to provide rental space for local traders. On 6 May 1859, the former reading room was leased as a shop to Druggist Thomas Owles, who removed the north window and replaced it with a door. From 1860—1887, the shop was leased on a series of 7-year leases to William Juby Coleman, Chemist and Druggist, James Floyd, Chemist and Druggist, John Pettit, upholsterer and Josiah Frederick Paul, Bookseller, before its conversion to a Mayor's Parlour and Committee Room in January 1892.

The Town Hall also continued to perform its civic functions. In January 1885, for example, free tea and cake was served in both the Town Hall and the neighbouring Corn Exchange to 2,400 *"children of the working classes residing in Bury St Edmunds between the ages of 5 and 12 ... each child bringing his or her own mug." (Meeres, 154)*. In July 1895 the General Election results for North West Suffolk (Stowmarket Division) were declared from the upstairs window.

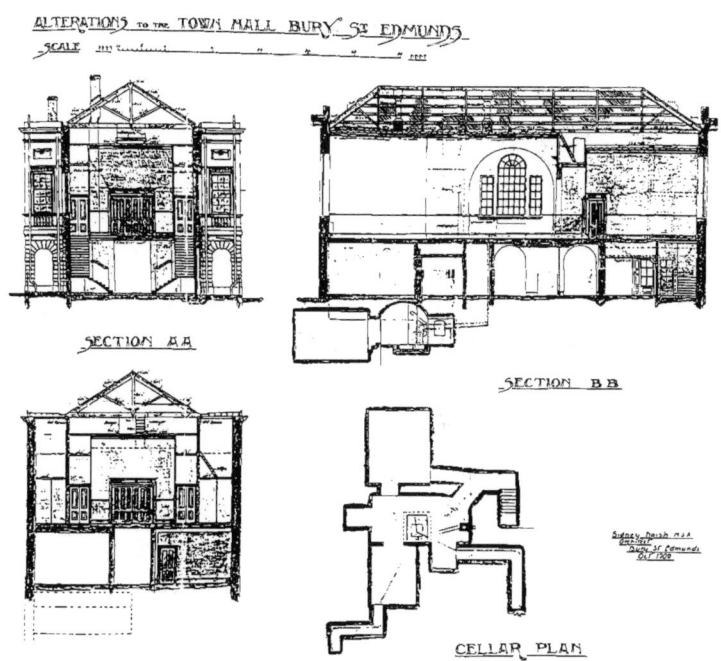

Naish alterations, 1909
(Suffolk Archives)

THE TWENTIETH CENTURY AND TODAY

ON 31 MARCH 1908, the upstairs room and roof of the Town Hall were severely damaged by fire, thought to have been caused by a poorly-built fireplace. Curiously, the Town Hall fire occurred nearly three hundred years to the day since its medieval predecessor was destroyed in the Great Fire of Bury of 10 April 1608.

In September the following year the council approved plans by Abbeygate Street architect Sidney Naish to renovate the damaged building. This included rebuilding the roof as a single pitch, removing the theatre galleries (which had apparently survived Wilkins' dismantling of the theatre in 1819) and reinstating the stored trophy panels, removed in 1840. His drawings include for the first time a plan and elevation of the extensive cellars of the Market Cross. In June 1910, the first public meeting was held in the newly-repaired building.

During the early years of the Great War, the Town Hall was used for Military Service Tribunals, to hear appeals for exemption from military service on the grounds of a reserved occupation (such as farming, forestry or engineering), medical unfitness, hardship or conscientious objection. Many local farmers appealed for exemption for their sons, to prevent them being conscripted to the Western Front. Later in the war, the Town Hall replaced the Corn Exchange as Bury's Soldiers Club, providing servicemen with refreshments, games, reading and writing rooms by day, and hosting concerts and dances by night. Following the Armistice, at a public meeting in July 1919, the council announced details of the proposed Peace Celebrations, to be held in Bury on Saturday 19 July.

Town Hall meeting, July 1919
(Bury Past and Present Society K505 661)

In 1936, the building briefly housed the Bury Free Library, before this was moved to the neighbouring Art School in 1937. The following year, new council offices were opened on Angel Hill, and many municipal functions were transferred from the Town Hall.

However, the Town Hall was to play an important role during the Second World War. In July 1939, it was the control room for a highly-complex exercise, when nine bombers from RAF Stradishall carried out a mock night-time air raid on the town, to test the readiness of its emergency services. This was coordinated from the Town Hall, where a team of volunteers received incident reports, alerted the relevant emergency services and plotted progress on a map of the town. When the telephone lines were reported as disabled, messages were carried by runners from the Boy Scouts and Girl Guides.

ANNOUNCING
The Ministry of Food's
Official Demonstrations
AT THE
TOWN HALL, Bury St. Edmund's
ON
THURSDAY, 9th MAY, 3 p.m.
FRIDAY, 10th MAY, 3 p.m.

Don't miss this opportunity of obtaining full information about War-Time Food.

DEMONSTRATIONS also at the
ELECTRICITY SERVICE CENTRE of
The East Anglian Electric Supply Co., Ltd.,
3a, CORNHILL, BURY ST. EDMUND'S.
Telephone 281

Ministry of Food poster, May 1940

This exercise proved a useful rehearsal for another potential purpose. The standing reports of the Royal Observer Corps Operations Room at the Guildhall indicate that, in the event of its destruction by enemy action, a fully-functioning reserve Operations Room was to be maintained at the Town Hall. It also served as a local office of the Ministry of Food, holding supplies of ration books and hosting public information events, such as the official demonstration of 'War-Time Food' in May 1940, four months after the introduction of food rationing.

During the 1950s and early 1960s, the Concert Room on the upper floor served as a badminton court, while hosting weekly dances and events such as cage bird fairs.

The Market Cross as a badminton court (O G Jarman)

In June 1969, the council approved a scheme by Marshal Sissons Architects to restore the original Adam plan, with the ground floor partially reopened in the arcaded style of the old

Market Cross. This work took place during 1970—71, with the archways on the west and north sides being opened up to create arcades and a new shopfront, designed by Bury architect Mark A Pawling, built within the west arcade. It was during this work that some of the timber beams of the original Market Cross, encased by the later Adam building, were again exposed. Following its restoration in January 1971, the building was once again renamed The Market Cross.

IN APRIL 1969, a Steering Committee had been formed to raise money for the creation of a new art gallery in the Market Cross, but had been unable to raise sufficient funds. In November 1971, a renewed appeal was launched by Sir John Wolfenden (then Director of the British Museum) to raise funds for an art gallery, concert hall and lecture room. This appeal proved more successful, and in April 1972 the Bury St Edmunds Art Gallery Trust was formed, with the objective *"to promote the best contemporary art, craft and design from Britain and abroad, and support the professional development of artists"*.

The interior of the building was restored in elegant Adam Style, and the new Bury St Edmunds Art Gallery opened on Thursday 9 November 1972. Its first exhibition was *Two Hundred Years of Suffolk Art*, featuring works by Gainsborough, Constable, Thomas Churchyard, the brothers Smythe, Alfred Munnings, Rose Mead and Alfred Blundell. Over the next two decades, under the curatorship of Sylvia Thomas, the Art Gallery hosted a lively programme of events, including the V&A touring exhibition *The House at Pooh Corner*, an exhibition of Henry Moore sculptures, lunchtime concerts and evening film shows.

Throughout the 1970s the ground floor of the building attracted graffiti and antisocial behaviour, although proposals to re-enclose it were rejected by central government until 1985, when it was temporarily enclosed by hoarding. In 1989 it was infilled, as a permanent extension to the building society which then occupied it, and since 2010 the entire ground floor has been occupied by a bookmaker.

The art gallery on the upper floor was renamed Smiths' Row Art Gallery (after a former row of market stalls) in 2010, but closed due to financial difficulties in November 2015. The building then reverted to being known as The Market Cross, a name it retains to this day. Since that time it has been only sporadically used, most recently as a creative arts, dance and events venue, which opened in April 2021 but closed its doors two years later.

The Art Gallery, 1970s (Pat Spillane)

Adam's Market Cross in 2024

THE FUTURE?

SO WHAT OF the future for Bury's Grade I Listed Market Cross, one of the town's most important landmarks?

This iconic building began life as a medieval preaching cross and corn exchange, before becoming Bury's first playhouse. It was remodelled as a theatre by one of Britain's foremost architects, and later became Bury's Concert Room, Town Hall and Art Gallery.

It currently stands with its upper storey locked and empty, and its ground floor in a use unsympathetic to its historical significance. It is a building whose architectural quality and cultural prominence marks it out for a renewed public or community role, so that both residents of Bury and visitors to the town can enjoy and once more take pride in it.

2024 marks the 250th anniversary of Bury Corporation commissioning Robert Adam to redesign the Market Cross. It would be highly fitting if this important anniversary were to be marked by the renaissance of *"the finest post-medieval building in Bury"*.

APPENDIX

OFFICIAL LIST ENTRY ON THE NATIONAL HERITAGE LIST FOR ENGLAND

MARKET CROSS (1076930)

FORMER PLAYHOUSE AND TOWN HALL, now an art gallery on the upper storey with offices below. Between 1774 and 1780. By Robert Adam, architect; built by Thomas Singleton, stonemason of Bury St Edmunds, who also carved the decorative panels. White brick with Ketton stone used for dressings on the upper storey above a rusticated ground storey.

EXTERIOR: 2 storeys; oblong cruciform plan; on an island site. The ground storey has semicircular headed arches on all faces and is partly open; some windows with glazing-bars. Doorways on the north and south fronts have a panel on each side carved in low relief with masks and emblems representing the Muses. The upper storey has all 4 principal faces treated in the same way with a Venetian window embraced by Ionic engaged columns supporting a frieze and pediment. On each side are plastered niches carrying Etruscan type stone ornaments. Stone panels above these niches have swags and paterae. All other faces have C19/C20 replacement small-paned sash windows set in moulded stone architraves, some with pediments on console brackets and some with cornices and ornamental friezes. All windows on the 1st storey have stone balustrading to the sills. The building is topped by a stone cornice with a stone band below.

INTERIOR: has undergone considerable changes and the upper room is now rather plain: plaster cornices with palmettes; 3 central bosses in the ceiling have acanthus-leaf decoration and a fluted outer ring with swags. Doors with 4 long moulded sunk panels. A fireplace, with detached fluted columns, decorated with plaster swags and garlands, is in Adam style but made of cast-iron. An exact double of this fireplace surround is in a principal bedroom at No.2 Angel Hill, now part of the Angel Hotel.

BIBLIOGRAPHY

PUBLICATIONS

Adam, R and J (1779) *The Works in Architecture of Robert and James Adam*, Volume II Part V, plates vi—vii

Ashby, G (1782) *A Description of the Ancient and Present State of the Town and Abbey of Bury St Edmunds in the County of Suffolk*

Bettley, J and Pevsner N (2015) *The Buildings of England, Suffolk: West*: Yale University Press

Bishop, P (1998) *The Sacred and Profane History of Bury St Edmunds*: Unicorn Press

Bury St Edmunds Art Gallery Trust (1997) *25 Years at the Market Cross*

Clifton-Taylor, A (1984) *Another Six English Towns:* BBC Publications

Defoe, D (1724) *Tour Through the Whole Island of Great Britain*: Penguin

Fiske, J (ed) (1990) *The Oakes Diaries: Business, Politics and the Family in Bury St Edmunds, 1778-1827* Vol I James Oakes' Diaries 1778—1800: Suffolk Records Society XXXII

Fiske, J (ed) (1991) *The Oakes Diaries: Business, Politics and the Family in Bury St Edmunds, 1778-1827* Vol II James Oakes' Diaries 1801—1827: Suffolk Records Society XXXIII

Garrioch, D (2019) Towards a fire history of European cities (late Middle Ages to late nineteenth century) *Urban History*, 46(2), pp202—224

Gautier, B (1998) 'The Planning of the Town of Bury St Edmunds: A Probable Norman Origin' in Gransden, A (ed) Bury St Edmunds Medieval Art, Architecture, Archaeology and Economy, *British Archaeological Association Conference Transactions XX*, pp81—97

Gibson, G M (1981) Bury St. Edmunds, Lydgate, and the N-Town Cycle *Speculum* 56, 1, 56—90

Green, D P M (undated, accessioned Suffolk Archives 1992) *The Market Cross, Bury St Edmunds: a History*

Grice, E (1977) *Rogues and Vagabonds, or the Actors' Road to Respectability*: Terence Dalton, Lavenham

Haslewood, Rev F (1887) *Monumental Inscriptions at Bury St Edmunds, vol I*

Lansman, R (2014) 'God save our lord the King' in *Roaring Lions and Gasbags: Bury St Edmunds in Twenty-One Amazing Stories*, 42-5: Bury Heritage Guides

Mackintosh, I (1979) *Pit, Boxes and Gallery: The Story of the Theatre Royal, Bury St Edmunds*: The National Trust

Mackintosh, I (1983) 'The Rise and Fall of the Georgian Playhouse 1714-1830 – A Cautionary Tale' *Architectural Association Files* 4, 16-28

Masschaele, J (2002) The Public Space of the Marketplace in Medieval England *Speculum* 77, 2, 383—421

McCutcheon, E (1987) *Bury St Edmunds Historic Town*: Alastair Press, Suffolk

Meeres, F (2002) *A History of Bury St Edmunds*: Phillimore

Miller, C (2008) *By Particular Desire: The Theatre, Bury St Edmunds*: Theatre Royal

Morris, C (ed) (1982) *The Illustrated Journeys of Celia Fiennes, 1685-c1712*: Macdonald

Orbell, J (2017) *A Handsome and Substantial Building: A History of Bury St Edmunds Corn Exchange*: Taylor's End Press

Orbell, J (2021) *In Search of a Roof: Bury St Edmunds Buttermarket in the 1850s and the building of a covered market hall*: Taylor's End Press

Rosenfeld, S (1936) 'The Players in Norwich' *Review of English Studies* 12, 47, 285-304

Statham, M (1970) *Plays and Playhouses in Bury St Edmunds* (unpaginated typescript)

Statham, M (1988) *The Book of Bury St Edmunds*: Barracuda

Taylor, M (2018) *Bury St Edmunds in 50 Buildings*, 55-57: Amberley

Walker, A (1987) *Franz Liszt, The Virtuoso Years (1811—1847)*: Knopf Doubleday

ONLINE

Market Cross, Bury St Edmunds *National Heritage List for England* https://historicengland.org.uk/listing/the-list/list-entry/1076930?section=official-list-entry

Robert Adam (1728—1792) *Oxford Dictionary of National Biography* (ODNB) https://doi.org/10.1093/ref:odnb/105

Robert Adam: Neoclassical architect and designer *Victoria and Albert Museum* https://www.vam.ac.uk/articles/robert-adam-neoclassical-architect-and-designer

SUFFOLK ARCHIVES

Bury St Edmunds St James Parish Registers, Burials 1562—1800, Suffolk Green Books XVII, 55, 1 BUR 1916

Cornhill, Bury cuttings file

Theatre Royal Wilkins Deed-plan, 1819 E4291—18

Playbills, 1776—1802 HD 912

Photographs and Prints K511/402, K511/482, K511/483

SIR JOHN SOANE'S MUSEUM COLLECTION

Robert Adam Drawings Volume 38, 38—40

ACKNOWLEDGEMENTS

WHEN I FIRST came to Bury St Edmunds some twenty years ago, I was struck by the Georgian elegance of the town's Market Cross. I learnt that this fine neoclassical building was one of the lesser-known works of celebrated architect Robert Adam. Later, when training as a Bury St Edmunds tour guide, I became increasingly fascinated by its rich and sometimes surprising history. Later still, while researching the history of James Oakes' Guildhall Street house (designed by Adam's contemporary John Soane) and browsing the collections of Sir John Soane's Museum, I came across Adam's original pencil drawings of the Market Cross. This spurred me on to prepare a lecture on its history, which slowly and quite unintentionally grew into the present book.

In writing the book, I have relied heavily on D P M Green's slim but comprehensive book *The Market Cross, Bury St Edmunds: a History*, and all extracts from the Bury Corporation Minutes are derived from this invaluable source. I am most grateful for the helpful comments and advice I have received from Dr Pat Murrell, from my fellow tour guides Martyn Taylor and Terry O'Donoghue, and from Dan Clarke of Moyses Hall Museum, Sue Palmer and Flora Spens of Sir John Soane's Museum and all the staff of Suffolk Archives' Bury Record Office. My thanks also to The Victoria and Albert Museum, Sir John Soane's Museum, The National Portrait Gallery, Historic England, The Royal Institute of

British Architects, Moyse's Hall Museum, Suffolk Archives, Suffolk News and the Bury Past and Present Society, for permission to use their photographs. I should also like to thank Lorna Brookes of Crumps Barn Studio for her editorial and design skills and Wendy Horrex for her endless patience and support. Needless to say, any faults or inaccuracies in the book remain entirely my own.

ABOUT THE AUTHOR

ADRIAN TINDALL was born in London and studied archaeology at the universities of Sheffield and Bradford. He worked as a professional archaeologist for over forty years, including twenty as county archaeologist for Hereford and Worcester, Cheshire and latterly Cambridgeshire.

He has carried out fieldwork in East Anglia, the Midlands, Yorkshire, the North West, Wales, Orkney, Italy and Libya, and has for many years given talks to local groups, schools and adult education classes. He is a Fellow of the Society of Antiquaries and a Member of the Chartered Institute for Archaeologists.

Although now retired from professional archaeology, he remains a Trustee of West Stow Anglo-Saxon Village Trust. He lives in Bury St Edmunds and is an accredited Green Badge Tour Guide, an Associate of the Institute of Tourist Guiding and Chair of the Bury St Edmunds Association of Registered Tour Guides.